IF THIS PLAYSET IS RETURNED LATE
– BY EVEN ONE DAY –
A FULL REHIRE CHARGE IS PAYABLE

Samuel French — London
New York - Toronto - Hollywood

KISS OF DEATH

First performed at The Mill at Sonning Dinner Theatre on 17th May 2000, with the following cast:

Zoë Lang	Susie Trayling
Bernard	Michael Percival
Brocklebank	David Quilter
John Smith	James Staddon

Directed by Simon Williams
Designed by Jacqueline Hutson

CHARACTERS

Zoë Lang, a young actress
Bernard, a criminal psychologist
Brocklebank, Detective Superintendent, Special Covert
  Criminal Investigation Department
John Smith

The action takes place in an old, refurbished science
lecture room and in John Smith's derelict flat

Time — the present

Other plays by Simon Williams
published by Samuel French Ltd

Laying the Ghost
Nobody's Perfect

ACT I

Scene 1

An old but refurbished science lecture room

We have the impression that the room is remote and deep underground. The atmosphere of age is offset by the presence of a great deal of new technology. The room is shaped like an amphitheatre of sorts; the theatre auditorium forms the seating area. The room is windowless and sound-proofed, with sliding doors L *and* R, *operated by a remote control unit or by keypads next to the doors. There are desks, chairs, filing cabinets, telephones etc., a fridge and a recording console. A feature of the room is a large practical television monitor (or two smaller ones) linked to a practical hand-held video camera. Around the room are various other technical devices, remote controls and practical speakers. There are piles of files on the desks*

When the Curtain *rises the stage is in darkness*

Two sets of footsteps echo down a long corridor. A door clangs shut in the distance. A single set of footsteps approaches the room

The Lights come up

Bernard, a dour figure in very dark glasses, sits at a desk, writing on a clipboard. Brocklebank stands at the back of the auditorium, unnoticed as yet

One of the sliding doors opens electronically and Zoë enters. She is chewing gum

Bernard closes the door with a remote control. He does not look up at Zoë —yet; he remains immersed in the notes on his clipboard throughout the following

Zoë Is this it?
Bernard Yes.
Zoë This isn't much of a place.
Bernard No.
Zoë Do you know what is supposed to happen next?

Bernard No.

Zoë Are you with these people, then?

Bernard Yes.

Zoë But they don't tell you what's going on?

Bernard No.

Zoë Doesn't that strike you as being a bit daft?

Bernard No.

Zoë You're not a huge amount of fun to hold a conversation with, are you?

Bernard No.

Zoë You're quite happy with just the monosyllables?

Bernard Yes.

Zoë You don't feel like moving on from the yes and no scenario?

Bernard No.

Zoë Hm? Shall I leave perhaps?

Bernard Wait here.

Zoë Please.

Bernard Please. Wait here.

Zoë Wow — brilliant. Couldn't we in fact flesh that sentence out a bit? We could for instance have begun it with "I'm sorry for the delay but perhaps you wouldn't mind waiting here." Or: "I know you've come a long way" — three changes of train, a bus ride and a short walk in the rain actually — " and given up a lot of your valuable time to be here, but bear with us if you can …" Something like that would have been nice. Wouldn't it?

Bernard My job description does not include making conversation with you at this point.

Zoë No chit-chat then?

Bernard Not one of my duties, alas.

Zoë Alas.

Bernard Please sit down and wait. (*Pre-empting her*) Silently.

Zoë (*sitting down; robotically*) Order to sit accepted. Sitting in progress. Sitting completed. (*Pause*) You don't want to see my tits, then?

Bernard No.

Zoë Do you always wear dark glasses?

Bernard Yes.

Zoë Have you heard the story about the nun and the blind man?

Bernard Yes.

Zoë rises restlessly and peers into the auditorium

Zoë Hallo. Hallo. Is anybody there? I'm getting a little impatient.

Bernard Yes.

Zoë Cooeee! (*To Bernard*) Tell whoever it is I'm leaving. OK?

From the darkness at the back of the auditorium Brocklebank speaks quietly without moving

Brocklebank Stay where you are.
Zoë Hi, there.
Brocklebank Good-afternoon. You're Zoë Lang, are you?
Zoë Yes. With no "i". Lang with no "i". (*To Bernard*) No "i".
Bernard (*correcting his notes*) No "i" — pardon me, I'm sure.
Brocklebank I'm sorry your journey was so tiresome.
Zoë Have you been there all along?
Brocklebank There's a lot to be said for tranquillity, you know. You have the documents?
Zoë (*to Bernard*) She made no comment.
Brocklebank Very thorough. All right. "Now is the winter of our discontent."
Zoë "You know your Shakespeare."
Brocklebank "Am I really ...?" (*He laughs*) That's by way of being a joke.
Zoë Isn't that when people laugh?
Brocklebank Very prickly. Very right on. Gum out.
Zoë You don't think it's rather archaic, using Shakespeare for security?

Bernard hands Zoë a Post-It note; she uses it to get rid of her gum

Brocklebank I suppose it is, Miss Lang with no "i"; perhaps in future I'll use lyrics from the Spice Girls.
Bernard (*laughing*) "You know your Shakespeare." My! That is amusing.
Zoë So that's the formalities done.
Brocklebank More or less. I'm sorry you were kept waiting.
Zoë Are you?

Brocklebank comes on to the stage from the auditorium

During the following Bernard picks up the video camera

Brocklebank Yes. A little. Were you offered tea?
Zoë No.
Brocklebank Bernard.
Bernard Yes, sir?
Brocklebank Did you not offer Miss Lang tea?
Bernard No, sir.
Zoë We were too busy chatting away, weren't we?
Brocklebank Would you like some tea?
Zoë No, thank you. Why have I been brought here? What is this place?

Brocklebank It's the lecture room. We use it from time to time. It offers privacy and a certain atmosphere.
Zoë An ordinary office would have been fine with me.
Brocklebank The location is not in question. It's not for you to question the location. (*To Bernard*) Bernard, are you ready?
Zoë Yes, I'm ready.
Brocklebank Would you sit down, Miss Lang?
Bernard (*pointing to a specific chair*) There.

Zoë sits in the chair (possibly with her back to the audience). Brocklebank touches a switch and a spotlight comes up on Zoë. Bernard turns on the camera so that we see Zoë's image live and in close-up on the screen

Brocklebank Good. You don't mind the camera?
Zoë No.
Bernard Say something.
Zoë Your jacket needs taking to the dry cleaner.
Brocklebank I imagine you know why you are here?
Zoë It's work, I assume.
Brocklebank I wish I could say it was. Miss Lang — may I call you Zoë? ——

Zoë nods

— I'm afraid I have some bad news for you.
Zoë Oh yes?
Brocklebank We tried to reach you earlier. It's your child.
Zoë My child … (*She rises*) What are you saying? Has something happened to Joshua?
Brocklebank I am afraid so … Please sit down.
Zoë What has happened?
Brocklebank We did all we could.
Zoë (*after a pause*) He's dead. You mean he's dead? He can't be …
Brocklebank I'm so sorry. So very sorry.
Zoë (*sobbing*) I can't believe it. I just can't believe it …
Brocklebank I'm so sorry. We all are.
Zoë What happened? I thought it was going so well.
Brocklebank It was. He didn't suffer though. He's at peace. A sweet child. Would you like some tea? Bernard could fetch you a brandy perhaps.
Zoë You bastard …
Brocklebank I beg your pardon?
Zoë I told you it had to stop, but you wouldn't listen.
Brocklebank What are you talking about?
Zoë The Defronskzi trial.

Brocklebank The what? What are you saying?

Zoë I know what you're doing. I've seen the files.

Brocklebank (*moving to Zoë*) What files have you seen, Miss Lang?

Zoë (*quite overcome*) My baby ... My baby. You bastards. (*She pushes him away*) You people — you're nothing but a bunch of freaks.

Brocklebank I think you'd better explain yourself, don't you, Bernard?

Zoë You see, I have spoken to Martin at the Lab ... I know.

Brocklebank Martin was nobody. He was a plant.

Zoë A plant. I don't think so. I never gave my consent. I never signed the form. You killed him — you killed Joshua. (*She tries to avoid the camera*)

Bernard pans the camera to follow Zoë

Brocklebank Please control yourself. What's done is done. I offer you my deepest sympathy.

Zoë Turn that thing off. Turn it off. I'm going to destroy you. It's as simple as that.

Brocklebank Look ... I had no idea you knew so much.

Zoë I trusted you. You knew his immune system wouldn't take it. Didn't you? You killed him.

Brocklebank He died peacefully. In the end we had no choice.

Zoë I do. I have a choice. I'm going to put you behind bars, this whole laboratory is a fraud.

Brocklebank We are a government agency, remember. We are protected.

Zoë Then I'll track you down, Mr "Now is the winter of our discontent", and I'll kill you. Do you understand?

Brocklebank Look, we are prepared to be generous, you know, very generous.

Zoë Oh, yes ... Go on.

Brocklebank You are an attractive woman ——

Zoë *What*? Is that appropriate?

Brocklebank I don't see why not — you are very attractive.

Zoë Thanks to Dr Zeiglemann.

Brocklebank Zeiglemann?

Zoë It was he who reconstructed what was left of my face.

Brocklebank (*scrutinizing her*) Is that right?

Zoë Yes. After the explosion.

Brocklebank A terrible accident.

Zoë It was sabotage, as you well know.

Brocklebank Of course. He did a good job.

Zoë Thank you. My father's reputation was at stake.

Brocklebank Your father?

Zoë He was in "Thin Air".

Brocklebank "Thin Air"?

Zoë The Seventies rock group …

A buzzer goes off. Brocklebank switches off the spotlight

Bernard switches off the video equipment and makes notes on a clipboard

Bernard That's it. Time's up.
Brocklebank The fun and games are over.
Zoë (*checking her watch*) It's over? That's it. So soon.
Brocklebank You did very well. A high score. There's nothing like improvisation for sorting out the men from the boys.
Zoë The women from the girls. It was fun.
Brocklebank I liked her initiative, didn't you, Bernard?

Bernard nods

(*Looking at Bernard's notes*) I see you gave her a nine for initiative. That's praise indeed. Nine. The baby thing was very out-on-a-limb. You moved it forward well. The laboratory idea — very quirky. The grief, the Defronskzi stuff — very droll, very sharp.
Zoë Yeah, well, a lot of it seemed pretty flaky.
Brocklebank Not for you, surely, a student of the famous Tuck Van Meiser in New York?
Zoë It was only a three-month course.
Brocklebank (*consulting the notes*) In Improv. and Free Thinking. I'm impressed … What have we got? … Nine for imagination. And a very rare ten for speed of reaction. Well done. The plastic surgery and the explosion was going a bit far. That can be dangerous.
Zoë We were running out of time.
Brocklebank Only a seven for resolution. And on the sexual level — your response was weak. I offered the compliment, made an opening and you diverted.
Zoë It was a pathetic compliment. "You're an attractive woman." Hardly assertive.
Brocklebank It's not my skill that's under scrutiny here. We marked it as a missed opportunity.
Zoë It's your party.
Brocklebank I liked the aggression though, the "I'll track you down and kill you" stuff. Very good. Eight.
Zoë Thank you.
Brocklebank (*looking at the score*) Now is that kind? For general turn-out — three.
Zoë (*to Bernard*) That's quite ruined my day.

Brocklebank Oh dear, you won't like what he's put under "Any other comment".

Zoë (*snatching the clipboard; reading*) "Spunky attitude and peachy tits" — you are a dysfunctional little tosser, aren't you?

Brocklebank Settle down. It's altogether a very good score. Forty-two out of a possible fifty. Well done.

Zoë Am I supposed to care?

Brocklebank Don't you?

Zoë It may be forty-two out of fifty in your book. In mine it's four hundred pounds in cash for "an improvisation workshop".

Brocklebank It's a failing, you know, this need you have to control the agenda. Patience is a virtue not only in a woman, but in a person and more especially in an agent.

Zoë I've done what I was paid for, I don't have to sit here and listen to you two jerk off with your score cards and stuff.

Brocklebank So nicely put. You've been recruited before, you know the deal.

Zoë Is that what this is?

Brocklebank As if you didn't know. As if she didn't know. Of course it's a recruitment. What did you think it was — an audition for *Puss in Boots*?

Zoë No sign of Dick, though.

Bernard (*chuckling*) No sign of Dick. Humorous.

Brocklebank You take pot luck on these recruitment sessions.

Zoë I can look after myself.

Brocklebank You like adventure then?

Zoë That's not quite what I said.

Brocklebank It's a leap in the dark coming to this kind of assignation?

Zoë Yes, it is.

Brocklebank You can't complain then if the circumstances don't suit you.

Zoë I've never given up the right to hand back my fee and walk out. (*She moves to the sliding door*)

The door remains closed

Open the door. (*Pause*) Open the frigging door.

Bernard Language, language.

Brocklebank (*to Bernard*) You're right — she is spunky. (*To Zoë, very amiably*) Miss Lang — Zoë — please sit down. Sit. (*He shakes Zoë's hand*) George Brocklebank. Detective Superintendent Special Covert Criminal Investigation Department.

Zoë You have ID?

Brocklebank Listen to her. Don't make me laugh. ID? You wouldn't know ID if it bit you on the nose. (*To Bernard*) Show her.

Bernard passes her some documentation from his clipboard, including a photograph of Brocklebank

Zoë (*looking at the photograph*) It's a very old photograph.
Brocklebank I'd say that was impudent, wouldn't you, Bernard? I hate bad manners.
Zoë Old but distinguished all the same. (*To Bernard*) And who are you?
Brocklebank He's Bernard Heal.
Zoë I asked him.
Brocklebank His name is Bernard Heal.
Zoë Is that right?
Bernard Yes. That's my name. You can call me Mr Heal.
Zoë Do I get to see your paperwork?

Bernard produces his paperwork with a flourish. Zoë looks at it

What did the MOD need you for, then, Bernard V. Heal? Your conversational skills? What's the V for?
Bernard Valentine.
Zoë Is that right? (*She picks up the video camera, switches it on and points it at Bernard*)

We see Bernard's face on the screen, staring at us. He still wears his dark glasses

Let's put the boot on the other foot. What sort of a man are you, Bernard Valentine Heal?
Bernard Imperturbable. That's what I am. Imperturbable.
Zoë Is that right? In my book, you're a nerd.
Bernard You're too kind.
Zoë Why don't I want to trust you? A criminal psychologist, a boffin and four sets of initials to prove it. Let's have a look at you, shall we? I'll tell you what sort of man you are, Bernard Valentine Heal. You're the sort that gets quite a long way up my nose.
Bernard Oh! I am sorry.
Zoë What is it with you? Are you shy or what? Perhaps you don't like women, is that it, Mr Heal? What's with the bins? Huh? What have you got to hide, I wonder.
Bernard I do not like to be observed. I like to observe without being observed. Is that so wrong? I hide my eyes for your benefit, to save you —— (*He takes off his dark glasses*)

We see Bernard's face in close-up. His eyes are completely white. The effect shocks Zoë

(*Growling into the camera*) Embarrassment.
Zoë (*shocked*) I'm sorry. I'm so sorry ... I didn't think ... (*She switches off the video camera*)
Bernard (*of the dark glasses*) They are not just for the rich and famous. They are for those of us scarred or injured.
Brocklebank In the course of duty.
Zoë I'm *so* sorry.
Brocklebank It's not for you to question his credentials, Zoë. Believe me as nerds go, he's pretty sharp. (*He takes a bottle of water from the fridge*) Do you want some water? (*He tosses the bottle to Zoë*)
Zoë (*catching the bottle*) Thanks. (*She drinks*)
Brocklebank Anyway, Miss Lang with no "i", you are ideal for our purposes — (*to Bernard*) isn't she?

Bernard nods

Zoë And they are?
Brocklebank We'll come to that. (*He studies Zoë's papers*) The results of your medical are quite satisfactory. One or two interesting features there ... (*He chuckles*) And ... (*He picks up a very distinctive file from the desk and studies it*)

Bernard watches Brocklebank carefully and shakes his head to indicate "Not now"

(*Thinking better of mentioning the file*) Your Mensa score is very reasonable. Better than average. (*He reads; then*) I'm curious that you refused the lie detector.
Zoë That's what I do, it's part of the job. I tell lies, I pretend to be other people. You don't judge that with electronics.
Brocklebank Fair enough.
Zoë Plus the bloke in charge was a dork.
Bernard You didn't take to Eric then?
Zoë No.
Brocklebank You've been doing a lot of security work, industrial surveillance? Does that mean espionage these days?
Zoë "A rose by any other name ——"
Brocklebank "——would smell as sweet". ... Some undercover stuff for the CID and a stint with the Narcotics boys. How was that?
Zoë It beats temping.
Brocklebank Their report says you function well under pressure. It says you're cool and thorough.
Zoë (*to Bernard*) No mention of peachy tits then.
Brocklebank It says here you broke a felon's arm last year?
Zoë Yes.

Brocklebank Are you into martial arts?
Zoë No. I threw a wok at him.
Brocklebank Not exactly rolling in money.
Zoë I get by.
Brocklebank Bernard.

Bernard hands Brocklebank a paper from Zoë's file

(*Reading*) One thousand eight hundred and thirty-seven pounds overdrawn.
Zoë Don't I get any civil rights along the line?
Brocklebank Of course you do. How rude of me. Well ... (*He puts away the very distinctive file*)
Zoë What's that? What is that file?
Brocklebank Private is what it is. Very private.
Zoë If it concerns me, I'd like to see it.
Brocklebank I don't think so. To business. (*He pauses. To Bernard*) Do the names.

Bernard picks up several files and places them, one by one, on the desk. There are photographs and news cuttings in the files

Bernard Julie Pearson, Anne-Marie Mayo, Hayley Foster, Judy Aykroyd ...
Brocklebank And Caroline Bryce ... Mean anything to you?
Zoë (*after a long pause; appalled*) Let me go. I want to leave. I'm leaving.
Brocklebank Please don't.
Zoë Tell me this isn't what I think it is.
Brocklebank I can't do that. I can't tell you that.
Zoë They were all murdered, weren't they?

Brocklebank nods

By the same man?

Brocklebank nods

A serial killer?

He nods

That's who you are after?

He nods

What is it they call him in the papers?

Brocklebank ⎫
Bernard ⎬ (*together*) The Surgeon.

Brocklebank They call him the Surgeon.

Zoë (*holding a press clipping*) The Surgeon — that's right. He mutilates his victims. Dismembers them or something.

Brocklebank Disembowels actually. You don't want to hear the details.

Zoë (*reading*) "An ice-cool operator known to prey on young homeless girls." ... "The Ripper of our times." ... Caroline Bryce ... This was only three months ago ... "There are rumours that the notorious Surgeon is now playing a cat-and-mouse game with the investigating team, leaving false trails and then taunting them."

Brocklebank (*nodding*) The bastard.

Zoë "A police spokesman said they were currently pursuing several lines of inquiry." (*She looks up*) In other words you haven't got a clue.

Brocklebank No.

Zoë So who exactly are you guys?

Brocklebank We were co-opted independently on to the case five months ago. Our brief was to set up a new initiative, with a covert strategy of ...

Zoë The word you seem to be trying not to use is "entrapment".

Brocklebank You're ahead of me of course, Miss Lang.

Zoë You want to use me as bait?

Brocklebank I'd like to have sweetened the pill.

Zoë So what did you have in mind?

Brocklebank We've identified a possible contact point.

Bernard reads her a highlighted advertisement from a contact magazine

Bernard (*reading*) "Calling any lost sheep. Have you been a naughty girl? Are you lonely? Unhappy? Broke? Let me look after you. Call voice mail box 2237."

Zoë Lovely. So what's the deal?

Brocklebank We'd like you to pursue it.

Zoë Just like that?

Brocklebank First of all we set you up with a comprehensive alias.

Zoë Is that necessary?

Brocklebank Yes. We want you to match the kind of thing he's looking for. He double-checks every applicant. If there's the smallest doubt about them the trail goes cold.

Zoë You mean you've tried this before?

Bernard reacts uneasily

Brocklebank (*with a glance to Bernard*) No. And secondly we need to protect your identity. In the event of us drawing a blank we don't want him tracking you down — subsequently.

Zoë You have nothing on him?

Brocklebank Not a thing — not a print, not even a whiff of DNA. The psychology people have given us a personality profile but it's sod-all use. We've got nothing except a pile of case histories.

Zoë So there I am, the bait, his ideal victim; then what happens?

Brocklebank Having established contact we'd like you to proceed to a meeting. You'd be thoroughly monitored.

Zoë Wired for sound.

Brocklebank Yes. We'd be there as close as possible to — see what happens.

Zoë Waiting for him to confess. Or for him to attack me.

Brocklebank Your safety will be our top priority.

Zoë That's a comfort. And you really think he'll buy it?

Brocklebank We reckon so.

Bernard "Where the bee sucks, there suck I / In a cowslip's bell I lie."

Brocklebank Shut up, Bernard.

Zoë Will I be armed?

Brocklebank No.

Zoë I do have a licence.

Bernard We know.

Zoë Supposing I say no.

Brocklebank We have budgeted for you to have a two-tier payment. Double your previous fee for the operation and the same again if and when the Surgeon is arrested and convicted.

Zoë Hm. Clear of tax?

Brocklebank Be reasonable — we're supposed to be the good guys.

Zoë ponders

Zoë I've got nine points on my driving licence.

Brocklebank I think Operation Tyger Tyger could run to a clean licence. Don't you, Bernard?

Zoë Operation Tyger Tyger?

Brocklebank The poem. It's his calling card. The Surgeon uses it as his trade mark. He plays games …

Bernard "Tyger, tyger, burning bright
            In the forests of the night?
            What immortal hand or eye ——"

Brocklebank Thank you …

Bernard " ——Could frame thy fearful symmetry? ——"

Brocklebank (*stronger*) Thank you, Bernard. By the way, I think she may have been right about that jacket.

Zoë This isn't strictly kosher, is it?

Brocklebank There's a wee element of pork, yes.

Zoë Go on.

Brocklebank We're a very small *ad hoc* unit with a single objective. The Surgeon.

Zoë How small?

Brocklebank At the core of the operation, three.

Zoë You two and ... ?

Brocklebank DI Jerry Collingwood. We are covered by level five security.

Zoë I noticed.

Brocklebank We have access to every police resource and all data facilities.

Zoë (*re her file*) I noticed.

Brocklebank Perforce we are operating in extreme isolation.

Zoë I noticed.

Brocklebank As a consequence we are being allowed a little latitude with our approach. Isn't that right, Bernard?

Bernard nods

Zoë They're turning a blind eye.

Brocklebank The means justify the end.

Zoë The means are me — cosying up to a psychopath.

Brocklebank That's about it — yes. He must be caught. He's got to be stopped.

Zoë What sort of time frame are we on?

Brocklebank Tight. He must not be given time to claim another victim. We'd like to start work tomorrow with your prep and briefing. There's a lot to be done; the success of this operation is in the detail.

Bernard hands Zoë a fat folder. She checks it

Zoë What's this?

Brocklebank It's all you need to know about Natasha Campion. Your alias.

Zoë Who is she?

Brocklebank A drop-out from Southampton University. A loner, a loser, a crack-head desperate for funds.

Zoë Good victim material.

Brocklebank Exactly. You've done a bunk from rehab. and are on the streets.

Zoë (*looking at a photograph*) And this is her?

Brocklebank She's two years younger than you, same height, near enough the same weight — obviously not that fit. We'll have to change your hair.

Zoë Natasha Campion ... The lost sheep goes stalking the tiger ... (*She pauses*) See you tomorrow morning.

Zoë shakes hands with Brocklebank

Bernard escorts Zoë towards the exit

Bernard (*as they go*) "Where the bee sucks, there suck I ..."

They exit

Brocklebank produces his mobile phone, dials and then speaks into it

Brocklebank (*into the telephone; quietly*) Collingwood? It's me. ... Yes. ... A very good candidate. Zoë Lang with no "i". ... She's volatile but we'll just have to live with it. The training is crucial. ... Absolutely. That's your responsibility. There will be no history repeating itself. ... *Il faut casser des oeufs pour faire une omelette.* It's French, Collingwood. You have to break eggs to make a fucking omelette. (*He laughs and then disconnects*)

The Lights fade to Black-out

Scene 2

The same. Three days later

When the scene begins the room is in darkness. Bernard and Brocklebank sit facing the video screen(s). A video of Zoë as Natasha plays on the video screen(s). She looks quite different, with changed make-up and hair

As the video proceeds, the Lights come up to reveal Bernard and Brocklebank listening and watching

Zoë (*on the screen; talking into her mobile*) Hi. My name is Natasha, Natasha Campion. I — er — saw your ad. Re. the lost sheep thing. And I was wondering if you could help me ... (*She becomes distraught*) I've been so stupid — and I don't know which way to turn ... I've made such a mess of everything ... Sorry. I've got a mobile you could call me on, but no address ... 0751 554 4432. ... I don't expect you'll call back anyway. (*She sobs brilliantly*) Bye. (*She disconnects. Very brightly, to the camera*) Was that pathetic enough for you, Bernard? Has it brought a lump to your throat? *Throat* ... (*She giggles*)

Brocklebank turns off the recorder/video machine with a remote control

Brocklebank She's good. She's very good. Poor little Natasha. Downtrodden and woebegone.

Bernard Still no response though.

Brocklebank It's been what, three days? He'll call. How could he not, with bait like that?

Bernard I hope he's not checking her out just yet. Not too thoroughly. How is she doing?

Brocklebank With the prep. and training? Very well, there's a lot of it, mind. She's not quite ready. Where is she?

Bernard (*picking up the very distinctive file*) Have you been through this with her yet, the Uncle Gareth stuff?

Brocklebank No. Do we need to? Does she have to be put through all that?

Bernard It's why she's here. It's what gives her that edge.

Brocklebank The old iron in the soul syndrome? (*Reading the file*) Gareth Brodie ... Six years wasn't enough. They should have put him away for life ... Let's leave it. What's the point in using it?

Bernard Because it is the darkest secret she guards. It is a memory she has spent twelve years in therapy trying to wipe.

Brocklebank (*referring to the file*) And four days facing the bastard across the courtroom ...

Bernard Her psychiatrist's report should be sacrosanct. We need to see how she'd react.

Brocklebank Why?

Bernard It's where she's weak. It could break her.

Brocklebank It's too brutal.

Bernard That's the whole idea.

Brocklebank Not yet. She's not that resilient.

Bernard Then let's abandon the whole plan.

Brocklebank No. We've got to go ahead.

Bernard Regardless?

Brocklebank Do you have a problem with that?

Bernard I wonder how Canute felt as the waves reached his feet. Was it only his face he thought of saving?

Brocklebank You are as mad as a snake, Bernard.

Bernard There's a girl's life at stake. And this time, my friend, you will be held accountable.

Brocklebank I don't need reminding, Bernard.

Bernard This time there will be no doctoring of the truth. No sweepings under the departmental carpet.

Brocklebank That's already been agreed.

Bernard Collingwood knows what's happening, then?

Brocklebank Yes, yes, yes.

Bernard Are you sure?

Brocklebank Of course. How could he not?

Bernard And you trust him?

Brocklebank That goes without saying.

Bernard Say it anyway — for me.
Brocklebank For God's sake, Bernard. Collingwood is solid. OK?
Bernard Solid? How solid, why solid?
Brocklebank I *have* him OK. The details are under lock and key.

Bernard turns the camera on Brocklebank and switches on. We see Brocklebank's troubled face in close-up on the screen for all the following

Bernard Let's make this official shall we?
Brocklebank (*into the camera*) As you wish.
Bernard (*as a voice-over for the camera*) She should have had the Red Code File.
Brocklebank No. There is no need. Not yet.
Bernard And I still say it was an error of judgement not telling Zoë about Caroline Bryce.
Brocklebank It's not relevant. Caroline hadn't been tested under stress. She had no experience with role playing. We were outmanoeuvred, out-played.
Bernard This isn't a game.
Brocklebank I think to him it is.
Bernard What we have here is a maniac killing young girls. Remember that.
Brocklebank Whoops! Silly me, I nearly forgot. (*He flares up*) I screwed up, I know that, Bernard. Caroline was working directly under my instruction and still he got her. Just like that, from under our noses ... I wake up in the night remembering it, hearing his voice, that evil synthetic bloody voice.
Bernard The voice of Damocles. I thought we were working on a need-to-know basis.
Brocklebank We are. Zoë doesn't need to know Caroline was a police agent. Soon we'll catch the bastard and that will be that, OK? And I for one will be able to sleep quietly. A nice long quiet sleep.
Bernard Good; and in the meantime, I'm merely registering a demur?
Brocklebank A demur, Bernard?
Bernard About your *modus operandus*.
Brocklebank What the hell do you know?
Bernard I know the rules. And I'm watching you. Remember that.
Brocklebank (*blocking the camera lens*) Turn that thing off. Listen, you may not like me, Bernard, I can live with that. I don't like you a great deal either. We have to work together, all right?

Bernard turns the camera on himself. We see his face now, in close-up, huge on the screen

Bernard I'm sorry to hear I'm not your type. All I'm doing is registering my concern — my reservations. (*He switches the camera off*)

Brocklebank A very smart move; you're a canny bastard.
Bernard Thank you.
Brocklebank It's just a training exercise, Bernard, that's all. *Remember that. An exercise. She must be ready.*

A buzzer sounds. Brocklebank opens the door with the remote

Zoë enters. She is now Natasha Campion, as we have seen on the screen — made up, made over. She carries a bag — Zoë's own, not Natasha's

Zoë (*with a slight accent*) Is this all right, gentlemen? Was this how you see her, Natasha — call me Tasha — Campion?
Brocklebank Very good. Just right. Turn round. She doesn't need to sound too down-market. (*To Bernard*) What do you think?
Zoë Give us your best grunt of approval, Bernie.
Bernard You look the part. She looks the part. A real waif.
Zoë A victim.
Brocklebank A good blend of punk and frailty. The Surgeon likes frailty.
Bernard That's what the profile suggests.
Brocklebank The Surgeon likes modesty.
Zoë He dissects it with a scalpel.

Zoë produces "Natasha"'s mobile and places it on the desk

He still hasn't rung. He hasn't taken the bait.
Brocklebank He will. He'll take it. We have work to do. (*Handing a file to Bernard*) Here, you take her through it.
Bernard Birth date?
Zoë August twenty-second, 1980.
Bernard 1980. So you are?
Zoë Twenty-three.
Bernard Weight?
Zoë Fifty-eight kilos.
Bernard Birth weight. Birth weight, Dumbo.
Zoë Six pounds four ounces.
Bernard Father's middle name?
Zoë Henry.
Bernard Family dog?
Zoë Caesar.
Bernard Granny Ma's address?
Zoë Thirty-seven Lancaster Avenue, Basingstoke.
Bernard Correct. Your first boyfriend's name?
Zoë Barnie Watling.
Bernard Blond and blue-eyed?

Zoë He was West Indian.

Bernard Your GCSEs were in …?

Zoë Two English, History, Geography, General Science, Media Studies, French …

Bernard And? … And?

Zoë Er … Religious studies.

Bernard Your best friend was …?

Zoë Bella Wilkins.

Brocklebank Wilson. Bella Wilson. It's not good enough, Zoë.

Zoë *Zoë?* Who's she? Who is Zoë? I'm Natasha.

Brocklebank Good. Well done.

Bernard You've had your tonsils out, yes?

Zoë No.

Bernard When did you have glandular fever?

Zoë The summer of 1997.

Bernard How long have you been a junkie?

Zoë I've been a registered addict for eighteen months.

Bernard How much is a gram of crack?

Zoë Twenty-five quid.

Bernard And who is in charge of your programme at the Ashworth Rehabilitation Centre?

Zoë Dr Amanda Jeffries. It's not Ashworth, it's Harmsworth. The Harmsworth Rehabilitation Centre.

Bernard Of course — silly me. When were you confirmed?

Zoë I wasn't.

Brocklebank You were.

Zoë It didn't mean anything to me.

Brocklebank Not good enough. June eighteenth 1991. If you don't know the bloody answer, what do you do?

Zoë Attack.

Brocklebank So, when were you confirmed?

Zoë Look what the hell is this? Some kind of religious quiz?

Brocklebank That's better. Stay sharp.

Bernard Blood group?

Zoë Rhesus Negative.

Bernard Birth sign?

Zoë Leo.

Bernard Mother's maiden name?

Zoë Jenner.

Bernard Your favourite drink?

Zoë Bacardi and Coke.

Brocklebank You're with the police, aren't you?

Zoë Is that what you want? I once shagged a traffic warden — does that count?

Bernard You're a fake.
Zoë Yes. I am.
Brocklebank What?
Zoë I've never done this before. I've never done this kind of gig.
Bernard Is that right?
Zoë I'm desperate ...
Brocklebank Take your clothes off.
Zoë After you.
Brocklebank Are you a tart or what?
Zoë Bog off.

"Natasha"'s mobile rings. They all freeze. Bernard turns a remote button so the telephone conversation plays over speakers

Bernard exits during the following (to trace the call)

Brocklebank It can only be him. Are you all right?
Zoë Yeah. (*Into the phone; as Natasha*) Hallo.
John Smith (*voice-over*) Hallo. Is that Natasha Campion?
Zoë (*into the phone*) Yes, it is.
John Smith (*voice-over*) You rang my voicemail. I had placed an advertisement.
Zoë (*into the phone*) Oh, yes of course. The lost sheep thing. You said you could help.
John Smith (*voice-over*) That's right. I like to help young girls. Young women who are in trouble. Helpless young innocents who need a guiding hand.
Zoë (*into the phone*)What are you, a charity then?
John Smith (*voice-over*) Don't be a tease, Natasha.
Zoë (*into the phone*)I'm not a tart or anything.
John Smith (*voice-over*) I never said you were. It's a quite harmless arrangement.
Zoë (*into the phone*)You pay?
John Smith (*voice-over*) A modest remuneration. We all have our foibles, don't we?
Zoë (*into the phone*) What sort of foibles?
John Smith (*voice-over*) Innocent ones. For instance I would need you to wear — red. A red dress. Bright red knee-length. Do you understand?
Zoë (*into the phone*) Yes.
John Smith (*voice-over*) By the way, do your parents know you've run away from Harmsworth Rehabilitation Centre?

Zoë is freaked by his knowledge. Brocklebank urges her on

Zoë (*into the phone*) How did you know about that?

John Smith (*voice-over*) I know all about you.

Zoë (*into the phone*) Oh yeah?

John Smith (*voice-over*) Oh yeah. I'm very thorough — gentle mind — but thorough.

Zoë (*into the phone*) No, I haven't spoken to my parents. I'm on my own.

John Smith (*voice-over*) Where are you?

Zoë (*into the phone*) A friend's house — a squat.

John Smith (*voice-over*) Good. Here's what we'll do, Tasha — may I call you Tasha?

Zoë (*into the phone*) Yes …

John Smith (*voice-over*) Listen carefully, Tasha, I want you to go to Paddington Station where I'll call again, in say fifty minutes. I want to hear the sound of the station in the background. Is that clear?

Zoë (*into the phone*) Yes.

John Smith (*voice-over*) You will collect a package.

Zoë (*into the phone*) Will I? How?

John Smith (*voice-over*) I'll call again to explain once you're there. The package will contain recorded instructions.

Zoë (*into the phone*) Instructions?

John Smith (*voice-over*) Directions to my flat. And the keys to get in.

Zoë (*into the phone*) You won't be there? How polite is that?

John Smith (*voice-over*) You will arrive first.

Zoë (*into the phone*) Why's that?

John Smith (*voice-over*) Weren't you taught not to trust strangers, Tasha? (*He laughs*) I shan't be far behind you. I look forward to meeting you.

Zoë (*into the phone*) I didn't catch your name.

John Smith (*voice-over*) No, you didn't, did you? It's Smith. John Smith.

Zoë (*into the phone*) Is that right?

John Smith (*voice-over*) Yes. Paddington in forty-eight minutes.

Zoë (*into the phone*) And how will I know it's you?

John Smith (*voice-over*) By a swift process of elimination, Tasha, you'll know it's me. Bye-bye.

There is the sound of John Smith hanging up. Zoë disconnects. A silence

Zoë That was definitely him?

Brocklebank Yes.

Zoë Well, John Smith scores a perfect ten for weird.

Brocklebank And for thoroughness.

Zoë This is a lot different to anything I've done before, you know — buying dodgy gear off a fence or being a decoy at a drugs bust.

Brocklebank Zoë, we'll be there with all the back-up, you won't be put in any danger beyond ——

Zoë The call of duty. I mean, is he creepy or what. Just how far am I supposed to let things go with him?

Brocklebank Far enough for us to get the case on the desk of the CPS. We need proof. As soon as we've got the bastard nailed we'll be in there. (*He produces a small box from his pocket and removes a tiny radio microphone in the shape of a brooch from it*) I'd better show you how to put this on.

Zoë I'm pretty wired as it is.

During the following, Brocklebank attaches the brooch microphone to Zoë

What kind of range do these things have?

Brocklebank Half a mile if we're lucky. We'll be nearer than that.

Zoë And how fast can you people move?

Brocklebank Pretty damn fast.

Zoë It doesn't take long. To get murdered. I tell you I'm scared shitless. Can I call for help on this thing? (*She indicates the microphone*)

Brocklebank We'll know when. If you need to, use the poem to alert us.

Zoë Tyger Tyger?

Brocklebank (*adjusting the microphone*) Any line from it and we'll be there.

Zoë Will you?

They are very close. There is tension between them

Brocklebank I'm sorry about last night.

Zoë Regrets so soon?

Brocklebank I'm old enough to be your father.

Zoë I thought that was the whole point. Do you have a problem with that — in the cold light of day?

Brocklebank Yes, I do. (*He turns his head away*)

Zoë "The dirty old man turned his head away, unable to meet the young nymphet's calm steady gaze ..."

Brocklebank I took advantage of you.

Zoë Is that what happened? Was I drunk?

Brocklebank No.

Zoë Were you?

Brocklebank No.

Zoë These moments happen, George, they come with no baggage, no history. They have no future.

Brocklebank Elegantly put. It wasn't appropriate under the circumstances.

Zoë Come on ... I'm a damaged worthless screwed-up human being. We have a lot in common.

Brocklebank Don't say that.

Zoë We all have our needs, George, and we all have the power of veto. "Georgie Porgie, pudding and pie, kissed the girls and made them cry ..."

Zoë kisses Brocklebank sensually. He remains immobile. She inflicts a minor pain, a bite or pinch

Brocklebank Ah ... "When the boys came out to play, Georgie Porgie ran away." It's an empowerment thing with you, isn't it?

Zoë Empowerment ... What are you like?

Brocklebank Cleverer than you know — that's what I'm like.

Zoë What do they say about people who live in glass houses ... ?

Bernard's voice comes from the intercom

Bernard (*voice-over*) It's generally a sound idea if they don't throw stones.

Brocklebank That's the trouble with bugging devices — you have to watch out for the buggers.

Zoë Exactly.

Bernard (*voice-over*) I thought you'd be glad to know it's working.

Zoë Exactly. A girl has to cover her arse.

Brocklebank Is that what you were doing?

Bernard (*voice-over*) Consider it well and truly covered, Miss Lang.

Brocklebank Against what?

Zoë Betrayal, compromise — the *News Of The World*.

Bernard (*voice-over*) No trace on that call, it was made on a brand new mobile purchased this morning in Brent Cross. Do I gather Tyger Tyger is in "go" mode?

Brocklebank (*into the intercom device*) Yes, Bernard, it is.

Bernard (*voice-over*) Then I'll be waiting for you in the Provisions Office, Zoë, to kit you out.

Zoë What with?

Bernard (*voice-over*) A red knee-length dress for starters.

Brocklebank All Natasha's stuff. Her purse, student ID, stuff like that.

Zoë Right. (*She puts down her own bag*) I'll leave Zoë with you then.

Brocklebank (*nodding*) Good luck. Or do you prefer "break a leg."?

Zoë Good luck is fine. (*In the door*) Be there.

Zoë exits

Brocklebank dials a number

Brocklebank (*into the phone*) Collingwood? ... Yes. Fine. ... In thirty-seven minutes. I'll see you there. Good luck. ... All right then: break a leg.

(*He hangs up. He is troubled. Quietly, to himself*)
    When the stars threw down their spears
    And water'd Heaven with their tears:
    Did he smile his work to see?
    Did he who made the Lamb make thee?

Black-out

SCENE 3

During John Smith's following speech the set changes to a derelict flat, airless and dank, stripped bare of character and possibly leaking. The badly-fitting door has a fan light above it; there are cracked boards over the windows. There is a curtained area with cupboards in it US. There is a table with a script in a folder on it. A sound system features prominently. There is a note on the floor and, unseen at first, a nondescript holdall or Gladstone bag under the table

From the darkness we hear the voice of John Smith; the sound is crackly, as if coming from a cassette recorder

John Smith (*voice-over*) Hallo there, Tasha, you see it pays to plan things properly, doesn't it? Leave the station and take a taxi. Give the driver the address on the yellow Post-It. Do not talk to him. Say nothing. On reaching the destination disembark; the fare will be seventeen pounds fifty. Give him the enclosed twenty pounds and tell him to keep the change. Wait until he is out of sight and then walk south for half a mile to number thirty-seven, a house called Newlands — there's a green sign outside. You should not, repeat *not*, have been followed. Enter the building and go down to the basement door. Use the Chubb and then the Yale.

The Lights come up dimly on the flat interior, later the same day. It is raining hard outside. We hear distant thunder throughout the scene, and the odd flash of lightning

Zoë enters with a wet umbrella. She is wearing a red dress and the brooch microphone and is carrying a bag

Zoë turns the feeble lights on and looks around her. She sees the note and picks it up

Zoë (*reading*) "Welcome. I hope you like it. At least we'll have some privacy. ... In the centre drawer of the table is a cassette. Take it and put in the sound system, please."

Zoë is about to say something into her brooch microphone but thinks better of it—is the room bugged? She produces a tape, inserts it in the sound system, and switches on. This time the sound quality is much better

John Smith (*voice-over*) Well done. Welcome. Please make yourself comfortable. Just in case you're finding all this rigmarole a little strange, please let me assure you I wish you no harm.

Zoë looks about for signs of the man's presence

That's right, you have a good look round.
Zoë (*trying to stay cool*) I can't go through with this. Hallo. Is anyone there?

Zoë opens the curtains to the cupboard area. It is empty. She closes the curtains again. She goes to the door. It is now locked

During the following we see a torchlight shining faintly through the thin curtain material

Hallo. Let me out of here. (*Into the microphone brooch*) I've changed my mind, I want to leave. Hallo — hallo.
John Smith (*voice-over*) There are some biscuits in the tin — plain chocolate Hobnobs, if I'm not mistaken, are your favourites … You see, the truth is I've always found meeting people a problem — I never know what to say. So, in the folder on the table you will find that I've typed it all out, our conversation, just the way I want it. Will you please read from it?

Zoë takes the script from the folder and opens the first page. She reads along with his voice-over

Zoë (*reading to herself*)		"Perhaps you'll find it pathetic that a man such as I should have to
	(*together*)	invent the reality of his choice like
John Smith (*voice-over*)		this. Please bear with me, and read it as best you can …"

Zoë sits down

During the following speech John Smith emerges silently from behind the curtain. He is wearing a balaclava and surgical rubber gloves and carries his own copy of the script. He stands still, observing Zoë

"Obviously when you first see me, I may appear to you a little sinister. You must feel free to react accordingly, to let out a gasp perhaps or even a little shriek … "

Zoë (*unaware of him; reading*) "Oh hallo, you did give me a fright."
John Smith (*reading*) "I'm so sorry. Hallo, you must be Natasha, I'm so glad to meet you at last."

Zoë turns, sees John Smith, and screams, dropping the folder

During the following, lines read from the folders have quotation marks; lines "off-script" do not

Zoë Where the hell did you come from? What are you doing ... ?
John Smith Calm yourself. Calm yourself. I was giving you time to settle ...
Zoë (*freaked out*) Are you him — are you? Why are you ...? Can I ...? (*She flounders, backing away round the room*)

John Smith points to the folder. Zoë picks it up and finds her place

John Smith (*repeating his line*) "Hallo, you must be Natasha, I'm so glad to meet you at last."
Zoë "And you must be John Smith."
John Smith "Yes."
Zoë "I suppose everyone says what an unusual name. With a little laugh." I'm sorry. (*She repeats the line with a laugh*) "I suppose everyone says what an unusual name."
John Smith "Yes."
Zoë "How do you do. I must say you did give me a surprise there."

They shake hands. His hand is still be-rubbered

John Smith "I'm sorry. Do you like it here?"
Zoë "Oh yes. Very much. It's cosy."
John Smith "Good. You are just as I imagined you ——"
Zoë (*jumping her cue*) "Thank you."
John Smith (*halting her*) " —— apprehensive, fresh. Seemingly naïve."
Zoë (*correcting her cue*) "Thank you. You flatter me, I'm just a simple girl who has lost her ... " Look, can't we just do this whole thing without you hiding your face? It's really freaking me out.
John Smith (*angrily*) You want to see my face?
Zoë Yes. Is that so unreasonable?
John Smith When you see my face everything changes. Once you know my face — that's it.
Zoë What do you mean?
John Smith We go past the point of no return. Is that what you want? Is it?

Zoë No. OK. Leave it on, it's fine, the balaclava is good. Please don't take
it off.
John Smith No, it's coming off. You've spoilt everything.
Zoë No.
John Smith I'm taking it off now. (*He takes the balaclava off*)

Zoë covers her eyes

Look at me. Look me in the eye, Tasha. Come on. (*Loudly*) Look at me.

Zoë slowly opens her eyes. They stare at each other

John Smith (*pointing again to Zoë's script*) Can we carry on now? Where
were we? Yes ... (*He reads*) "You are just as I imagined — apprehensive,
fresh. Seemingly naïve."
Zoë (*resuming her role*) "Thank you. You flatter me ... I'm just a simple girl
who has lost her way in life."
John Smith "I would like to think I could help you, Tasha."
Zoë "You are so kind and masculine, John. I feel safe with you already. You
have such authority, such presence. You are like a lion."
John Smith "I'm very flattered. Would you like a Bacardi and Coke? That
is your preference, I believe?"
Zoë "Why, yes. Thank you."
John Smith "I always think planning ahead is a good idea." (*He produces
her drink, ready-poured, from behind the curtain and gives it to Zoë*)
"There."
Zoë "That's lovely." Whoops. (*She sips*) "That's lovely. Thank you."
John Smith "I did so want our first meeting to be real and natural."
Zoë "It is." (*Mispronouncing*) "*Que sera sera ...*"
John Smith (*correcting her*) "*Que*." (*Kay*) "*Que sera sera*." It's Italian.
What will be will be.
Zoë Right ... "*Que sera sera.*"
John Smith "I'm not being too forward I hope, too profound?"
Zoë "Oh no, I too am a fatalist, John. I believe in Fate. Everything we do is
pre-ordained isn't it? The choices we make are an illusion, aren't they?"
John Smith "That is so true, Natasha, we none of us have any real choice
about things: the way we live and the way we die ..."

They toast each other

"Cheers."
Zoë "Cheers." (*She sits down*)
John Smith "Please sit down."

Zoë gets up and then sits down again

Zoë "Thank you."

John Smith "You look animated, Tasha, dare I say excited."

Zoë "I am excited, John. I'm excited by the situation. Here we are together like two children."

John Smith "Your pulse is racing is it?"

Zoë "Yes, it most certainly is."

John Smith "I'm so glad. Your adrenaline is flowing is it? In your veins?"

Zoë "Yes. I feel quite warm. The palms of my hands are moist."

John Smith "Are they?"

Zoë "Yes."

John Smith Moist?"

Zoë "Yes."

John Smith "So here we are. Alone together. You're not afraid?"

Zoë "I trust you, John."

John Smith "You'll find me an honest man, Tasha, honest and tidy."

Zoë "I want to be looked after."

John Smith "You're a naughty girl, if I'm not mistaken."

Zoë "I know. I have naughty thoughts, John, but mostly I'm confused and helpless, aren't I?"

John Smith "Yes, that's how it seems to me."

Zoë "I am so lonely sometimes."

John Smith "Oh, Tasha, me too."

Zoë "I believe in Fate. In destiny."

John Smith "Me too. We have so much in common."

Zoë "Why don't you sit here, beside me?"

John Smith (*sitting*) "Thanks."

Zoë "As I was saying — I think we all have a dark side."

John Smith "Go on."

Zoë "I try to be good but like so many young girls these days I do have these unaccountable yearnings. These desires."

John Smith "Fantasies you mean? Oh yes, I understand. I understand young girls and their erotic fantasies." (*He comes off the script*) Their need to be conquered and punished ... You see, all the time they are pretending to be happy with their husbands, and with the life they lead in a leafy suburb, satellite dish and everything, badminton on Thursdays and the Neighbourhood Watch social evenings and going to Salcombe with the caravan on Bank Holidays — (*he becomes quite het up*) all that is as *nothing*. Because all the time their so-called hormones are dragging them into the mud — into filth and obscenity. All that stuff on the sheets, and his Nissan parked round the corner, and him telling me that she has needs. *Needs* that I didn't know about.

Zoë looks aghast at her script. John Smith pulls himself together and has to check his script

Zoë Er … I'm a bit lost … Shall we go from: (*she reads*) "I do have these unaccountable yearnings. These desires." (*She points to the page*) And then it's you …

John Smith I'm sorry. (*He reads again*) "Fantasies, you mean? Oh yes, I understand young girls and their fantasies. Do you have a particular one yourself, by the way?"

Zoë "I try my best to control impure thoughts but I'd like to dance with you, John."

John Smith "Now? Oh! All right, I'm not much of a dancer. What music shall we have? You choose."

Zoë "How about *Volare, Nel Blu di Pinto di Blu* by Dean Martin?"

John Smith "Good choice. I like that one too." (*He presses a button on the sound system and immediately the song is playing, as it's been set up to do so*) "Shall we?"

They dance rather formally, Zoë carrying her script

Zoë "You are a good dancer."

John Smith "We move as one, don't we?"

Zoë "This is so romantic."

John Smith "Your hair is very nice. Nice perfume too. Altogether attractive."

Zoë "Thank you. You look strong and manly."

John Smith "What are you thinking?"

Zoë turns the page. It is obvious that the script calls for a kiss

Zoë Hold on … "We hardly know each other, and yet …"

John Smith "What were you going to say, Tasha?"

Zoë (*with difficulty*) " Oh, John, kiss me."

They kiss, delicately and at some length. Zoë pulls away and puts the script on the table

Zoë I can't go on with this. I'm afraid I must go home. No offence or anything. Will you please open the door?

John Smith No. That's not right. That's not what you say.

Zoë I can't help that. I'm completely freaked out. I want to go home.

John Smith You don't have a home. Remember.

Zoë Unlock the door, please.

John Smith No. No, it can't end like this. (*Very reasonably*) We mustn't let this go wrong. Please stay. Please carry on …

Zoë considers her options. Her microphone. The man is probably controllable

John Smith turns the music off. During the following, he removes his tie

They are now unscripted again

Zoë OK. I'll stay. But without this, all right? (*She puts down her script*) Let's try talking normally. I want to talk to the real you.

John Smith You might not like the real me.

Zoë Let's take a chance.

John Smith For all you know I could be some kind of raving nutter.

Zoë I don't think so.

John Smith No?

Zoë You don't look like one.

John Smith What do you think they look like, then, these raving nutters, these so called psychopaths?

Zoë You tell me. I've no idea.

John Smith advances towards Zoë with his tie. Zoë freezes

John Smith (*sort of joking*) Fee, fi, fo, fum — I smell the blood of an Englishman …

After a brief hiatus they both laugh awkwardly

Zoë Something like that.

John Smith I mean there are so many of them about these days, aren't there?

Zoë Yes indeed.

During the following there are great bangs and rumbles of thunder and the odd flash of lightning

John Smith There's that one they're after. What's his name? The one who …

Zoë What? The one who what … ?

John Smith Disembowels his victims. Young girls.

Zoë The Surgeon. Isn't he known as the Surgeon?

John Smith Sssssh … (*A beat*) Don't say it, Tasha, don't say his name like that out loud. It spooks me.

Zoë I wonder what he's like.

John Smith Perfectly normal, I should imagine. An ordinary person like you or me.

Zoë Superficially at any rate.

John Smith A man who has had an unfortunate experience with a woman he thought was trustworthy, and all the time she was cheating on him ... Perhaps.

Zoë He's seeking his revenge, you think?

John Smith That would be a possibility.

Zoë He must be very clever — to have not been caught.

John Smith They'll never catch him, in my opinion.

Zoë No?

John Smith Just thinking about it has made my skin go all goose-pimply. How about you, Natasha, has someone just walked over your grave ...?

Zoë's mobile telephone rings. This is bad timing. She takes the phone out of her bag. John Smith grabs Zoë's wrist firmly and takes the mobile from her. It carries on ringing

John Smith Oh dear, oh dear, oh dear. Were you expecting a call?

Zoë No ... Perhaps it's my parents.

John Smith We don't want to be interrupted now, do we?

Zoë Let go of my hand.

John Smith (*answering the mobile. Sweetly*) Hallo. You want to speak to who? Natasha Campion? ... Oh dear, I think you must have a wrong number. ... Oh I am sorry, that is annoying. Is it? Well, I'm sorry to say there's nobody here of that name. ... (*He laughs convivially*) ... Then you must have mis-dialled, duckie. (*He hangs up*)

Zoë Who was it?

John Smith Said he was your Daddy. Daddy wanted to know where you were. Said he's lost your address.

Zoë Silly old Daddy.

John Smith He wanted to talk to Natasha Campion. I told him there was nobody here of that name. Nobody who answered to the name of Natasha Campion.

Zoë I heard you.

John Smith Aren't you going to ask why?

Zoë (*controlling her alarm*) Why?

John Smith Because we both know there is nobody here of that name.

Zoë I don't know what you are talking about. I am Natasha Campion.

John Smith Ha ha ha.

There is a pause. Zoë goes to her script and looks anxiously for her place

Zoë (*reading*) "Perhaps I'd better be going."

John Smith I don't think so.

Zoë checks the script deliberately

Zoë "Perhaps I'd better be going."

John just stares at her. She shows him the script

Zoë You say: (*reading his line*) "It's been so nice meeting you, Tasha, perhaps we can meet again."
John Smith Rubbish.
Zoë And I say: "I'd like that — perhaps you'll call me next week."
John Smith Rubbish. Rubbish. Rubbish.
Zoë "'Goodbye then." ... They kiss briefly. She exits.'

John Smith takes Zoë's script and tears it up. Thunder rumbles

John Smith No more play-acting. The game is over.
Zoë What do you mean?
John Smith Who are you?
Zoë You know who I am. I'm Natasha Campion.
John Smith You have abused my trust young woman. Abused it. I'm hurt and upset. I'm insulted.
Zoë You are sick in the head, do you know that, John Smith or whoever you bloody well are?
John Smith When cornered, what must we do?
Zoë What?
John Smith Attack. Isn't that right?
Zoë I'm Natasha Campion. And I am going home.
John Smith Sit down. You're not leaving.

During the following John Smith takes a white cloth from the Gladstone bag and lays it on the table

Zoë What's that?
John Smith Didn't you think I'd be curious to find out about you? Didn't you imagine I would investigate my new protégé?
Zoë I have nothing to hide.
John Smith She's such a nice helpful woman at the Harmsworth Rehabilitation Centre ... What's her name? Your doctor.
Zoë Dr Amanda Jeffries.
John Smith She was ever so helpful. When I suggested taking my niece Natasha for a cream tea along the coast, she said that would be no problem.
Zoë When was this?

John Smith Yesterday. A lovely sunny afternoon, the sun setting across a calm sea.

Zoë I don't believe you.

John Smith I didn't think you would. Tasha had beans on toast, do you hear? Baked beans with an egg on toast.

Zoë Oh yes. (*As an SOS*) Look, do you know that poem "Tyger Tyger burning bright".

John Smith I brought you a souvenir.

John Smith produces a thoroughly sealed, transparent plastic bag from the Gladstone bag. We can see that it contains offal, blood red, a mixture of solid matter and crimson slime

Zoë "What immortal hand or eye,
     Could frame thy fearful symmetry?"

John Smith Well done. So what have we got here, then … ?

Zoë keeps on with her recital — it is a frantic SOS to her back-up team

Zoë "In what distant deeps or skies
     Burnt the fire of thine eyes?"
  (*She sees the bag*) What is that?
     "On what wings dare he aspire?
     What the hand, dare seize the fire?"

John Smith As I, said a memento of her, a souvenir of Natasha Campion.

John Smith takes a knife from his pocket and cuts the plastic bag. The bloody contents spill out on to the white tablecloth

There is a clap of thunder

Zoë NO. No. No … (*She recoils, still trying to recite the third verse, gasping and screaming in horror*)
     "And what shoulder, and what art,
     Could twist the sinews of thy heart?
     And when thy heart began to beat,
     What dread hand? and what dread feet?"

CURTAIN

ACT II

The lecture room. The morning of the following day

When the Curtain *rises, Brocklebank and Bernard are sitting at the desk listening to a tape recording. Zoë's scream from the end of Act I is heard*

Brocklebank Play that bit again.

Bernard rewinds the tape and we hear the end of the last scene, with Zoë's recital of "The Tyger" in the foreground

Zoë (*voice-over*) "What immortal hand or eye,
      Could frame thy fearful symmetry?"
John Smith (*voice-over*) Well done. So what have we got here, then … ?
Zoë (*voice-over*) "In what distant deeps or skies
      Burnt the fire of thine eyes?"
   What is that?
         "On what wings dare he aspire?
         What the hand, dare seize the fire?"
John Smith (*voice-over*) As I, said a memento of her, a souvenir of Natasha Campion.

There is a clap of thunder

Zoë (*voice-over*) NO. No. No … (*Gasping and screaming in horror*)
         "And what shoulder, and what art,
         Could twist the sinews of thy heart?
         And when thy heart began to beat,
         What dread hand? and what dread feet?"
   You bastard … You killed her. You maniac, you bastard … You killed her. Get away from me … Help! *Help!*
John Smith (*voice-over*) Shut up. Stop screaming.
Zoë (*voice-over*) You're going to kill me too. You are him, aren't you?
John Smith (*voice-over*) Don't say it. Don't say it.
Zoë (*voice-over*) You killed her.
John Smith (*voice-over*) Get out.

Zoë (*voice-over*) What?

John Smith (*voice-over*) Get out of here. How dare you think you can come here and trick me. What are they doing, trying to trap me again? How stupid do you think I am? Clear off.

Zoë (*voice-over*) What?

John Smith (*voice-over*) Tell your superiors they are pathetic. Get out …

We hear a door opening and Zoë running down the street, still distressed and calling out. Bernard fast-forwards the tape

Brocklebank (*voice-over*) Zoë, Zoë are you all right? Zoë … Quick, get her into the car …

Zoë (*voice-over*) You bastard.

There is the sound of Brocklebank being hit hard, and his reaction

Brocklebank halts the tape. He bows his head on to the desk

Bernard It could have happened to anyone.

Brocklebank Shut up, Bernard.

Bernard He got away. I don't think we should blame ourselves. It's the risk you take with covert operations — skeleton manpower, equipment failure, et cetera, et cetera …

Brocklebank Shut up.

Bernard Natasha is OK. Zoë is OK. All in all things could have been a lot worse.

Brocklebank (*his head still down*) If you don't shut up, Bernard, I'm going to poke my Biro up your nose.

The telephone rings. Bernard answers it

Bernard (*into the phone*) Hallo. (*He puts his hand over the mouthpiece. To Brocklebank*) It's Collingwood.

Brocklebank I'll call him later.

Bernard (*into the phone*) He's in a meeting at present. … No, that's right, with his head on the desk, actually. … Very. We got the wrong address. … Yes, well, I've heard of cars with false number-plates but not houses. We were completely taken in. … Yeah yeah, like last time. … Things could have been a lot worse, though. … OK, keep your hair on. … The lab report confirms what? … (*He reacts*) Charming. … Zoë's fine. Back at home. … Yes, I expect she will. I'll let you know. … *Ciao*. (*He hangs up*)

Brocklebank Well?

Bernard The offal was pig's liver.

Brocklebank Lovely. What did he say?

Bernard He says it was a bummer.

Brocklebank Terrific.

Bernard I still say we don't *know* it was him. The Surgeon. It could be a copycat incident.

Brocklebank No. This is our man. It is him all right, waving two fingers at us. Again.

Bernard We have no hard evidence. No prints, no voice match, no hint of a confession.

Brocklebank No, nothing. Which is why it is him. It's his way of saying "Back off, leave me alone."

Bernard The way he did last time.

Brocklebank Will you shut up about last time, Bernard? Caroline Bryce wasn't the same thing at all.

Bernard Zoë should have been told about her all the same.

Brocklebank Why? To what bloody purpose?

Bernard Forewarned is forearmed.

Brocklebank I don't think so. What happened there was a one-off.

Bernard Yeah, they're still puzzling about that one down in the lab.

Brocklebank What?

Bernard How he managed to get the tracking device off her shoe.

Brocklebank Don't remind me. The point is — Zoë is now a busted flush.

Bernard Zoë as Natasha, yes. In her own right, though, a raw nerve has been exposed.

Brocklebank You're not suggesting the Red Code File?

Bernard nods

The Uncle Gareth option?

Bernard It would serve our purpose.

Brocklebank She has to be kept in the game. It's essential she pays another visit.

Bernard It'll take more than a strategic snog to persuade her this time.

Brocklebank Bog off, Bernard.

Bernard He who fights and runs away, lives to fight another day.

Brocklebank No more platitudes — you've had your quota for today.

There is a buzz from the entryphone on the desk. Brocklebank presses a button

Brocklebank (*into the entryphone*) Yes?

Zoë (*voice-over*) Good-morning.

Brocklebank Good-morning ... We weren't expecting you ... So soon.

Zoë (*voice-over*) I don't suppose you were. Open the door.

Brocklebank presses a button to let Zoë into the building

Brocklebank (*to Bernard*) Hell's teeth. Did we know she was coming? I thought she was under surveillance.
Bernard She was — is — was. You can't get the staff ...

Bernard opens the door to the room and Zoë strides in, silent and angry. She carries her bag

Brocklebank Hallo, Zoë. Are you all right? We were just saying that you did very well last night, very well indeed, considering the circumstances. Weren't we, Bernard?
Bernard Yes.
Brocklebank (*after a pause*) What I'm looking at is a very angry woman, right? You are furious. You look furious. Doesn't she, Bernard?
Bernard I can't see from here.

Zoë glances in Bernard's direction

Yes.
Brocklebank (*a "mea culpa"*) It was a bad night.
Zoë A bad night? I am locked in a basement with a fucking maniac begging for my life and you order the hit squad to break into the wrong house. Yes, you could call that a bad night.
Brocklebank He got away, yes. But nobody is hurt. Natasha is OK. You are OK ... It turned out to be pork liver, by the way.
Zoë Pork liver. Pork liver. What kind of a hoax is that?
Brocklebank Sick, pretty sick. But all in all — (*he includes Bernard in the following*) — things could be a lot worse.

Bernard whispers to Brocklebank, telling him to apologize

(*To Zoë*) What I'm trying to say is: I am sorry. Very sorry. I thought it went without saying — but of course it doesn't. I apologize abjectly. We both do.
Zoë I could have been killed.
Brocklebank Yes ... Is that why you came?
Zoë Partly.
Brocklebank You're not going to hit me again?
Zoë I might. (*She checks out the recording console*) I'd like to hear the tape from last night? Have you got it? There's something he said ... Just before he threw me out.

Bernard sets to work preparing the tape on the console

Zoë What did Collingwood have to say?
Brocklebank In police jargon — he said it was a bummer.
Zoë A kindred spirit. I'd like to meet him.
Bernard Possibly not.
Zoë You will be making a full report?
Brocklebank Of course.
Zoë You can spell "cock-up" then, can you?

Bernard presses a button. And the tape plays

Bernard Around here?
John Smith (*voice-over*) Get out of here. How dare you think you can come
   here and trick me. What are they doing trying to trap me again. Just how
   stupid do you think I am?
Zoë There ... Back.
John Smith (*voice-over*) "... trick me. What are they doing trying to trap me
   again. Just how ..."
Zoë There. He says "*again*". He says trying to trap me again. What's that
   mean? Hm? ... Explain that to me.

Brocklebank looks at Bernard. A decision is made

Brocklebank I think you're right, Bernard. Why don't you sit down, Zoë?
   Perhaps you'd like Bernard to make you some coffee?
Zoë Would that be your usual coffee, Bernard?
Bernard Yes.
Zoë (*taking a teabag from her bag and handing it to Bernard*) I'll have one
   of these, thank you.
Bernard There's no need to go all Helen Mirren on me.

Bernard leaves

Zoë I'm not going to like this, am I?
Brocklebank The truth is, Caroline Bryce was a police agent.
Zoë Caroline Bryce — who was killed.
Brocklebank Yes.
Zoë She was working for you?

Brocklebank nods

Brocklebank We managed to keep it out of the press. As far as they were
   concerned, she was ...

Zoë Just another victim …

Brocklebank Yes … We were totally outwitted. He set us a false trail, and we took it … We lost her.

Zoë What happened?

Brocklebank (*after a moment*) Somehow he managed to persuade her that he was a police agent, one of us, and that the whole thing was simply a training operation for her benefit.

Zoë A police agent? He persuaded her that he was in fact a cop — and she believed him?

Brocklebank Yes, as far as we can make out. He is a very cunning, plausible man. Anyway the audio link was turned off.

Zoë What did you do?

Brocklebank She still had her tracking beacon. We trailed them across country, ending up in Gravesend —where we raided a premises in which we found an old man happily …

Zoë What?

Brocklebank Re-united with his carrier pigeon. The tracking bug had been attached to a carrier pigeon … We were completely stymied. The next morning we found her in a motel room two blocks from here.

Zoë Dead?

Brocklebank Oh, yes — the usual ritual. He's not called the Surgeon for nothing. (*He can't speak for a moment*) When people tell me I'm taking this operation too personally — I tell them to look at the police photographs of Caroline Bryce in that motel room. I tell them to listen to his message.

Zoë (*after a pause*) Nevertheless you decided to have another go with me.

Brocklebank I saw no alternative. I'm sorry. I told you it was a highly covert operation.

Zoë (*shaking her head*) Can I hear it? The Surgeon's message.

Brocklebank If you must … I pretty well know it by heart. (*He inserts another cassette into the machine and activates it*)

We hear an anonymous electronic computerized voice

Computerized Voice Just who the hell do you think you are, Brocklebank? You and your stupid little charade. If you think I'm going to give myself up that easily my friend think again. Listen to this, George, listen to Caroline, your pathetic protégé, and then leave me alone. Is that clear?

We hear a distressed reading of a verse of "The Tyger" from the late Caroline Bryce

During the following, Bernard enters with a cup of herb tea for Zoë

Caroline (*voice-over*) "Tyger, Tyger, burning bright,
  In the forest of the night;
  What immortal hand or eye,
  Could frame thy fearful symmetry?"
Computerized Voice (*or John Smith*) Go on, Caroline, one more verse ...
Caroline (*voice-over, very afraid*) "In what distant deeps or skies
  Burnt the fire of thine eyes?
  On what wings dare he aspire?
  What the hand, dare seize the fire? ..."

Caroline screams. At the high point of the scream, Brocklebank turns the tape off

Brocklebank You must surely understand I had to avenge that.
Zoë Is that what a policeman does? What about detachment and impartiality, judgement and all that crap?
Brocklebank I'd like to do it for her. The point is Caroline trusted me.
Zoë Oh yeah. So did I. (*To Bernard*) Thank you. You could have told me.
Brocklebank I very nearly did. I wish I had. Bernard wanted me to tell you, didn't you, Bernard?
Bernard *Neque sempre arcum! Tendit Apollo.*
Brocklebank What the hell is that?
Bernard Apollo doesn't always keep his bow strung.

Bernard exits

Brocklebank Bernard has had a very curious life.
Zoë So?
Brocklebank That's why he sometimes appears to have his head up his arse.
Zoë Screw you George. Did you seduce her too?
Brocklebank No. (*Very contritely*) What can I say?
Zoë Nothing. There is nothing to say, you're a man obsessed and that's dangerous.
Brocklebank I can't let it go. I just want to stop him. Catch him. Lock him up ... Destroy him.
Zoë Yes, well, it's poisoned you.
Brocklebank Maybe it has.

A mobile telephone rings in Zoë's bag

Zoë (*aghast*) That's Natasha's mobile. I was going to hand it in.
Brocklebank Answer it.

Zoë (*getting the mobile phone out of her bag and putting it on the table*) It's him. It can only be him.

Brocklebank Answer it. *Please* answer it.

Zoë I can't.

Brocklebank Zoë, talk to him. Please.

Zoë answers the mobile. John Smith's voice comes from a speaker thanks to a device on Brocklebank's desk

Zoë (*into the mobile*) Hallo.

John Smith (*voice-over*) Hallo. Is that you, Natasha? Or should I say Zoë?

Zoë (*into the mobile*) How do you know my name?

John Smith (*voice-over*) You ain't heard nothing yet. I've just found a very interesting recipe for pork liver with cream and rosemary sauce I thought you might like.

Zoë (*into the mobile*) You bastard.

John Smith (*voice-over*) There's no crime in having a little joke, Zoë. After all you were having one on me, remember?

Zoë (*into the mobile*) What are the hell are you trying to do?

John Smith (*voice-over*) I think we have unfinished business, you and I.

Zoë (*into the mobile*) Let's leave it that way, you stinking little pervert.

John Smith (*voice-over*) You're not worried that I'll come and find you, then?

Zoë (*into the mobile*) Is that a threat?

John Smith (*voice-over*) More of an invitation. I don't want you lying awake at night imagining that I'll come a-knocking on your door in the wee small hours …

Zoë (*into the mobile*) You'd never find me.

John Smith (*voice-over*) At your home you mean? Flat Three, Thirty-Seven Mobolt Street … I know a lot about you.

Zoë lowers the mobile in horror. Then speaks into it again

Zoë (*into the mobile*) Listen you little runt, you arsehole …

John Smith (*voice-over*) Language …

Zoë (*into the mobile*) What's the point of all this?

John Smith (*voice-over*) The point is you are intrigued. You are disturbed that there was so much of Natasha in you. You enjoyed pretending to be a victim, didn't you? It was familiar territory, wasn't it, Zoë?

Zoë (*into the mobile*) Shut up.

John Smith (*voice-over*) It reminded you of the trust you once had in someone. A trust that was abused — as you were. Because deep down you're still a victim, an injured soul looking for another chance.

Zoë (*to herself; distressed*) No ... The past is the past ... We grow, we develop, we move on, we change ...
John Smith (*voice-over*) I don't think so, Zoë. You haven't changed. You're still that nine-year-old girl, all alone in the house. Where's Mummy? Where's Mummy gone? And he's coming up the stairs, isn't he? Slowly up the stairs. Creak. Creak. Who? Ask me who, Zoë?
Zoë (*apprehensively*) Who?
John Smith (*voice-over*) Uncle Gareth.

Zoë puts the mobile down and retreats. Brocklebank picks it up and listens

Hallo ... Hallo ... Zoë? Have I upset you? Are you there? Hallo ... Zoë, you have to face it — the past. It's always there, creeping up the stairs ... Ask George, he'll tell you. He knows about the shadows.

Brocklebank terminates the call. He moves to Zoë

Brocklebank Are you all right?
Zoë (*shaking her head*) It's stupid to think you're cured when you're only in remission. The abuse may be over but as the song says: the memory lingers on. All the symptoms are still there, dormant. All they need is a little nudge and there they are, fresh as new. All you've been doing through the years is papering over the cracks. (*She studies Brocklebank, calmer now*) What shadows, George? What shadows do you know all about?
Brocklebank They're papered over too. He's a cruel man. And very thorough.
Zoë As you'd expect of a surgeon. He should not have had access to my psychiatric notes. Doesn't it strike you as odd, George, him having my notes, my most private and confidential notes?
Brocklebank It certainly does.

There is a tense moment of stand-off

Zoë (*calling out*) Bernard. Bernard!
Brocklebank What are you doing?
Zoë Just checking. (*To Brocklebank; earnestly*) Look, hasn't the Surgeon having such information aroused your suspicion?
Brocklebank In what way?
Zoë It's all too — neat. Too close to home.
Brocklebank You think he could be a doctor or a psychiatrist?
Zoë Or a policeman?
Brocklebank (*weighing Zoë up*) No, we've been down that path.
Zoë What the hell other explanation is there?

Brocklebank I don't know.
Zoë (*shouting*) Don't you? Don't you?
Brocklebank There's no need to shout.
Zoë Yes there is. When you can't run away any more that's what you do —
you turn and shout as loud as you can. (*She picks up the mobile and dials
during the following*) You attack. You confront. You kick as hard as you
can ...
Brocklebank What are you doing?
Zoë Calling him back. I'm going to have him, I'm going to get him.

Brocklebank makes to speak

   (*Overriding him*) I'm going to be rid of him so I can move on ...
Brocklebank (*pleased*) A very interesting reaction. Go ahead then.

John Smith answers. Again we hear his voice, amplified

John Smith (*voice-over*) I knew you'd call back. I was waiting.
Zoë (*into the mobile*) I want to see you again.
John Smith (*voice-over*) I'm so glad. Where?
Zoë (*into the mobile*) I'll be at Paddington Station in forty minutes. Call me
with a plan like you did before.
John Smith (*voice-over*) That's fine with me.
Zoë (*into the mobile*) No secrets. No crap. No blood and guts or dancing this
time. Just you and me.
John Smith (*voice-over*) Sounds like a show-down. Are you cross?
Zoë (*into the mobile*) Forty minutes, Mr Smith. (*She hangs up*)

Bernard enters

Brocklebank That was very impressive. Now this time I think ...
Zoë No, there's no "you" in this. You goofed up. I don't trust you. This time
I'm doing it my way ... I'm the one who scored nine out of ten for
improvisation, remember.
Bernard And only seven for resolution.
Brocklebank We have to work together.
Zoë No we don't.
Brocklebank (*picking up the brooch microphone from the desk*) Come here.
Let's at least share the experience ...
Zoë (*quoting directly at him*) "In what distant deeps or skies
        Burnt the fire of thine eyes?"
Brocklebank (*attaching the bug*) We'll be there.
Zoë Oh, yeah. And this time I want to be armed.

During the following Brocklebank's actions contradict his words. He opens a drawer in the desk and produces a container which holds a small revolver and passes it over to Zoë. She understands his ploy; their conversation is probably being recorded

Brocklebank I'm afraid that's out of the question.
Zoë I have a licence.
Brocklebank I know, but I couldn't possibly authorize it.
Zoë (*checking the revolver and pocketing it*) Well, I'll have to do without one then.
Brocklebank You have to trust me.
Zoë That's the mistake I made last time. I'll see you later. Thanks for the tea, Bernie.

Zoë exits

Brocklebank Suddenly we are dealt four aces.
Bernard Isn't it what you'd planned?
Brocklebank It's an unexpected bonus all the same.
Bernard The Trojan Horse was an unexpected bonus too, wasn't it?
Brocklebank What are you on about?
Bernard Beware the Greeks bearing gifts.
Brocklebank You should see a doctor.
Bernard You know my views on orthodoxy.
Brocklebank I have to know if her nerve will hold. We're not dealing with a parking offender here, we dealing with a homicidal bloody maniac.
Bernard So "Tyger Tyger" is back on full stand-by. I'd better spread the word.
Brocklebank Yes. Do.
Bernard The make-or-break scenario.
Brocklebank That's right. It isn't a dress rehearsal this time. He knows, the Surgeon, he knows it's nearly over.
Bernard What?
Brocklebank The whole charade. He's ready to call it a day. To surrender.
Bernard You hope.
Brocklebank (*internally*) In his mind's eye he can already see himself in the dock — his head nobly bowed in submission. As he hears the verdict delivered he will meet the judge's gaze quite steadily, maybe even with a rueful smile ... (*He produces a bottle of pills from his pocket and takes some*)

Bernard studies Brocklebank

(*Miles away*) He's hollow inside — burnt out ... What in the hell are you looking at?

Bernard Are you all right?

Brocklebank You're thinking I've lost the plot. I don't care. It's no use telling me not to let it get personal, Bernard. It's never been anything else. Anyone who had been to the morgue and seen any of those girls: Julie Pearson, Hayley Foster, Ann-Marie Mayo, Judy Aykroyd or even Caroline — the poor wee lamb with a name tag on her toe and her belly opened up — would understand.

Bernard I did see them, and I don't.

Brocklebank We have two objectives, Bernard: to get him and to protect her.

Bernard In that order?

Brocklebank They go hand in glove. (*He checks his watch*) We haven't got long.

Bernard (*again mindful of the walls having ears*) I'll say nothing, then.

Brocklebank Very astute, Bernard, as always.

Bernard Beware of the Greeks bearing gifts, that's all. (*With a remote control, he zaps the door open for Brocklebank*)

Brocklebank (*heading for the exit*) Screw the Greeks.

Brocklebank exits

Bernard picks up his mobile and dials

Bernard (*into the mobile*) It's me. He's left. … Exactly, mad as a March hare. … I think we should let things run their course. … Oh yes, he's given her the gun all right. She actually asked for it. The shoot-out was always on the cards; the Surgeon, it seems, is not going to go quietly. (*Chuckling*) Que sera sera …

Black-out

SCENE 2

The windowless, derelict flat. Forty minutes later

There is evidence that a police investigation has taken place. A glass of water stands on the table, as does John Smith's mobile phone

When the Lights come up, John Smith sits in the room, slowly pulling on a pair of surgical gloves. He sits still for a time in meditation

During the following recitation the Lights fade to black-out

John Smith "What the hammer? What the chain?
     In what furnace was thy brain?
     What the anvil? What dread grasp,
     Dare its deadly terrors clasp?"

Time passes. The Lights comes up again

John Smith is in the same position. There is a noise beyond the door. Hearing the noise, John Smith stealthily opens the door

Zoë enters. She is wearing her brooch microphone and carrying her bag

John Smith closes the door behind Zoë. There is a long silence

John Smith (*less of a nerd now*) We meet again. Come in.
Zoë The criminal returns to the scene of his crime.
John Smith The victim too. There's the novelty.
Zoë The one place they'd never suspect.
John Smith I wasn't born yesterday. What made you come?
Zoë Curiosity.
John Smith Well, we know what it did to the cat. Would you like some water?
Zoë No, thank you.
John Smith Curiosity about me?
Zoë You had no right to that information.
John Smith You mean about Uncle Gareth?
Zoë Yes. Uncle Gareth. Gareth Barlow.
John Smith But if it wasn't for him you wouldn't be here. He gave you the anger that gives you the courage. Am I right, Zoë?
Zoë That information was private. Absolutely and for sure, private.
John Smith So it must have seemed. They hold you hostage to information like that. It's why they picked you, Mrs Paranoid. They knew that your past gave them a point of access, a lever if you like. It's how they work, you see. What else?
Zoë Am I curious about?

John Smith nods

     Last night was bogus. Completely artificial.
John Smith You certainly were. Poor little Natasha Campion. You must have worked quite hard on your role.
Zoë And you on yours. The neighbourhood freak, the nerd with the balaclava, the rubber gloves and stuff: that wasn't really you.

John Smith The pig's liver was fun, though, wasn't it?
Zoë It was terrific.

John Smith locks the door. During the following he moves behind Zoë

John Smith You didn't have to kiss me, you know.
Zoë It was in the script.
John Smith You enjoyed it.
Zoë Natasha was faking it.
John Smith I don't think so.
Zoë That's just a male fantasy. Who are you?
John Smith You know who I am.
Zoë Say it.
John Smith The Surgeon. You think I'm the Surgeon. You've got me. Well done. Your mission is over. Agent Lang with no "i" picks up her fee and rides off into the sunset.
Zoë You are the Surgeon.
John Smith If you were sure about that, you wouldn't be here. If Brocklebank had any hard evidence he wouldn't have had to use you as bait, would he?
Zoë No. You play games.
John Smith I'm deadly serious.
Zoë A double bluff.
John Smith I've lost count. I want to be left alone, Zoë. I've proved my point, I've had enough. Like you I have my demons to confront.
Zoë You killed Caroline Bryce.
John Smith Now that was fun. Game on. George should never have sent her, mind, gift-wrapped like that ... (*He produces a silk tie, loops it round Zoë's neck and rubs it gently to and fro*) But she was nowhere near as much fun as you, Zoë. Peachy tits notwithstanding.
Zoë (*puzzled by the phrase*) What? Let me go. You're hurting.
John Smith Why can't Brocklebank realize that I don't *like* the idea of being captured?
Zoë Please let me go, I'm sorry, please let ——
John Smith Put your GK9 on the table.
Zoë What?
John Smith Your microphone, clever-clogs, put it on the table. (*He takes off Zoë's brooch microphone and speaks into it*) Isn't this where I get a crazy look in my eye and confess. Shall I break down and reveal why I hate women?
Zoë I don't understand. (*She whispers in terror, perhaps to the microphone*) Help. Please, wherever you are, please — help me.
John Smith (*checking his watch*) Poetry time.

Zoë What?

John Smith *Tyger Tyger.* Perhaps this time it'll work better ... Off we go
... Go on! "Tyger tyger ..."

*John Smith makes Zoë hold the brooch microphone, keeping the tie round her
neck*

Zoë   "... burning bright
         In the forest of the night;
         What immortal hand or eye,
         Could frame thy fearful symmetry?"

John Smith *(into the brooch microphone)* "In what distant deeps or skies
         Burnt the fire of thine eyes!"

Zoë   "On what wings dare he aspire?
         What the hand, dare seize the fire?"

John Smith *(with great faked alarm)* Christ Almighty ... Put that gun away.
I didn't know you were armed. Don't shoot, Zoë, give me that gun, come
on. *(He jerks the silk tie)*

*Zoë screams. In the middle of the scream John Smith drops the brooch
microphone into the glass of water. Zoë crawls away from John Smith in near
hysteria*

John Smith *(immediately different)* I'm sorry about that. Look I'm not going
to harm you. Are you all right? *(He moves to help her)*

Zoë *(shaking and bemused)* What? Keep away from me.

John Smith I haven't got long — Brocklebank will be here in a moment.

Zoë What are you talking about?

John Smith My name is Jerry Collingwood, DI. This is all part of a covert
training exercise.

Zoë What? What are you saying? None of this is real ... ?

John Smith Exactly.

Zoë You're a policeman? Part of the operation? You are Collingwood?

John Smith Yes.

Zoë What proof can you offer?

John Smith You never met him did you? *(He shows Zoë a card)* I'm here
under cover. As you are.

Zoë You are lying. You are the Surgeon.

John Smith I'm not. I tell you — he's still out there.

Zoë Bollocks. This is a trick.

John Smith It's not. Think about it. It's all a charade for your benefit. How
else could I have so much detail on you? Why should they put you through
all this? It was set up to put you to the test.

Zoë No, no, no … Why?

John Smith When they lost Caroline Bryce they knew that they'd have to have a much smarter agent to put in her place, someone whose nerve wouldn't fail.

Zoë A training exercise? You expect me to believe that you're working for Brocklebank? You're not Collingwood. You can't be.

John Smith I am.

Zoë Screw you. He warned me that you'd try this.

John Smith Who, Bernard?

Zoë Brocklebank. He said you did the same thing with Caroline. You told her the same lie, that you were part of the team. And she fell for it.

John Smith (*puzzled*) He told you that ? The thing is I was expecting you to be armed.

Zoë What?

John Smith I thought you had a gun. I was expecting you to use it. That was why I said that stuff about "Don't shoot — put the gun away."

Zoë What?

John Smith I was trying to help. You have to use the gun, Zoë … That's the point. I thought you must have lost it.

Zoë picks up her bag and produces the gun from it. She points it at John Smith

Zoë Well, I haven't.

John Smith Ah. Good. You see they had to know that you'd use it if you had to.

Zoë Don't worry about that. Stay where you are …

John Smith moves

I said stay where you are.

There is a loud knocking on the door. In the distance we hear police sirens etc.

John Smith (*shouting*) Who is it? (*To Zoë*) As if we didn't know.

Brocklebank (*through a megaphone; off*) This is the Police. Detective Superintendent Brocklebank. Let me in. Zoë, are you there? Are you all right?

Zoë Yes. I am.

Zoë keeps John Smith covered with the gun throughout the following

John Smith George, tell her who I am.

Brocklebank (*off*) Tell her what? We all know who you are. John Smith, I'm arresting you. Open the door and come out.

John Smith George, stop it. The thing is over. She's got me covered with the gun, the mission is completed.

Brocklebank (*off*) Zoë, are you all right?

Zoë Yes. He's telling me he's DI Collingwood. Is that true?

Brocklebank (*off*) Of course he's not, for Christ's sake. I warned you he might try something like that.

Zoë This isn't a training exercise … ?

We hear police activity outside and see a blue flashing light etc.

Zoë keeps the gun pointing at John Smith throughout the following. The following lines can overlap a bit

Brocklebank (*off*) Of course not. Is it likely?

Bernard (*shouting; off*) Zoë, you mustn't believe anything he says. Open the door.

John Smith Zoë, he's lying. You must believe me. Just listen to me a moment …

Zoë No … Open the door. Give me the key.

John Smith Zoë, trust me. Please, please, I know you have no reason to, but you must trust me now.

Zoë (*after a beat*) Stay where you are – don't come near me. Put the key on the floor.

Brocklebank (*off*) We're coming in …

John Smith rushes at Zoë and she is forced to pull the trigger. John Smith falls to the floor with blood coming from his mouth

Zoë I've killed him … Oh my God.

Brocklebank (*off*) Zoë, are you all right? Get this door open.

Zoë (*calling out*) I'm coming — it's all right.

Zoë, sobbing and shaking, drops the gun, takes the key from John Smith, stumbles to the door, opens and unlocks it. Blue police lights can be seen flashing outside

Bernard enters followed by Brocklebank, who is wearing gloves. Possibly a uniformed policeman appears at the door as well

Zoë collapses in Bernard's arms. Brocklebank attends to the corpse

Bernard It's all right. We're here. You're safe.

Brocklebank He's dead.

Zoë Dead … I had no choice, he was coming at me.

Brocklebank We've got our man. The Surgeon is dead ... Are you all right?

Zoë (*distraught*) He was going to kill me ... I had to ...

Brocklebank Exactly — what else could you do? You had no choice. You did very well. (*To Bernard*) Bernard, take her to the car — get her to the doctor.

Bernard Right.

Brocklebank Get her sorted. Make sure she's looked after. I'll see you later, Zoë, when we get through here. (*He calls off*) Sergeant — escort them out of here.

Bernard (*with his arm round Zoë*) Come on, pet. It's all right.

Brocklebank Tell the boys I'll call them as soon as I'm ready. OK? (*To Zoë*) I'll see you later.

Zoë takes a last look at the corpse and then allows Bernard to take her off. They exit

Brocklebank closes the door. He takes in the room slowly. He seems satisfied

Unseen by Brocklebank, John Smith stirs and crawls towards the unsuspecting Brocklebank

Brocklebank (*without looking round*) You did well, Jerry. I sometimes worry about your aptitude for schizophrenia.

John Smith (*wiping the "blood" from his mouth*) My preference would have been for something subtler. All that stuff with blanks and blood capsules is so messy.

Brocklebank Subtler, my arse. We had to take her to the wire.

During the following, Brocklebank picks up the revolver. He produces a silencer and attaches it to the gun

John Smith There are no ethics in your book, are there? It never crossed your mind to tell her the truth.

Brocklebank What fucking good did the truth do for Caroline?

John Smith You are a hard taskmaster, George.

Brocklebank We're not dealing with some half-arsed flasher in the park, you know. I can't let her loose on the target unless she's ready. I don't want that bastard catching us with our pants down again.

John Smith She did very well. She's a good girl. Gutsy.

Brocklebank You weren't so bad yourself, Jerry. You tapped into something there. Some of that stuff you were giving her was in the Jack Nicholson class. Especially with that damn poem. Spooky.

John Smith Just following orders, George.

Brocklebank I needed to know she could handle things when push comes
to shove.

John Smith I didn't see why you had to have her kill me.

Brocklebank She has to believe that she shot you.

John Smith But why didn't you tell her just now?

Brocklebank Tell her what, Jerry?

John Smith That I'm alive and well — me, Jerry Collingwood, your
colleague.

Brocklebank All in good time, Jerry.

John Smith She still believes she shot me.

Brocklebank Yes.

John Smith I still don't see why.

Brocklebank Because people would talk if it was me.

John Smith You who what?

Brocklebank Who shot you. The trick was getting you to play along.

John Smith I do as I'm told. You're the boss.

Brocklebank I know. You're a real team player.

John Smith So you get her to fire a blank and then I squash a blood capsule,
what's the deal?

Brocklebank The deal? Obviously Zoë will get off with self-defence. But
for you the prospects aren't so good. You see, Jerry, I need a real corpse.
(*He points the gun at John Smith*)

John Smith What are you doing?

Brocklebank Obviously I'd like to take time to explain it all to you but sadly
with pathology being what it is these days, I have a bit of a problem with
the time of death thing. I only have a margin of seven or eight minutes to
play with. And the boys are waiting outside.

John Smith What are you saying?

Brocklebank What am I saying? I'm saying goodbye, Jerry.

John Smith Goodbye?

Brocklebank That's right.

John Smith Why would you do this?

Brocklebank The Surgeon has to be stopped. Nobody is safe as long as he
is still around.

John Smith You? It's you, George. The Surgeon. ... You're him. It was you
all along.

Brocklebank laughs

I thought we had discounted the idea of it being one of us, an inside job.

Brocklebank Yes, Bernard took some persuading, though, didn't he?

John Smith So you're fitting me up — is that it?

Brocklebank It's all perfectly recorded back at base — your confession, the
strangulation, the poem, the fatal shot ... I've got you, Jerry.

John Smith Is this for real, George?

Brocklebank nods

This isn't a training mission at all? I'm just being used as a … (*He carefully picks up his mobile phone and — unseen — presses the redial button*)
Brocklebank Fall guy. Yup. It's time the Surgeon was caught. Justice has to be seen to be done … Put that (*he indicates the mobile*) down.

John Smith puts the phone down

You see the public needs a perpetrator. And you're it, Jerry, I'm afraid. You're the sacrificial lamb. No blanks this time. Real blood too.
John Smith This was all part of your plan, the built-in double-cross.

Brocklebank nods again

You bastard.
Brocklebank As I said earlier, "*Il faut casser des oeufs pour faire une omelette*". It's just a question of knowing which eggs to use.

Brocklebank shoots John Smith, who falls to the floor

(*Checking John Smith's pulse*) That's something that can't be faked. A star performance. (*He tidies up the scene, replacing the gun where it should be. He looks around, pleased with his work, and speaks into a device*) Tyger Tyger to HQ. I want forensics and the medics and ambulance here immediately …

Black-out

SCENE 3

The lecture room. The following evening

The following voice-over speech covers the set change. During the speech, the telephone rings

News Reader The serial killer known as the Surgeon has been shot dead in a North London basement flat as the Police attempted to arrest him last night. Earlier reports suggested that the wanted man was holding captive a potential victim at the time of his death. A police spokesman would neither confirm or deny the rumour that the dead man was himself an undercover police officer. And finally Ken Livingstone announced today that the …

The Lights come up. Bernard is on stage. He turns off the radio news and answers the telephone

Bernard (*into the telephone*) Detective Superintendent Brocklebank is not available for comment at the moment.... I cannot give you that information. ... If that were the case it would of course be classified as self-defence. Or justifiable homicide. ... Her name is not being released at this time. ... No comment. ... Yes, you could say that — a great relief. ... Thank you.

Brocklebank enters

Bernard I thought you'd gone home.
Brocklebank No. Who was that?
Bernard Three guesses.
Brocklebank The press? Have they found her?
Bernard No, thank God. We've been trying to contact her all day.
Brocklebank Stupid little fool. I hope she's not thinking of going to the tabloids. Where the hell can she be?
Bernard She could be suffering some kind of trauma; poor kid could be in shock.
Brocklebank It was a mistake to release her. How did she seem when she left?
Bernard Not too bad. The medical team gave her the all clear. And when the forensics boys had finished she collected her stuff and I let her go home.
Brocklebank Stuff? What stuff?
Bernard Her bag and her mobile and things.

Brocklebank ponders this. During the following Brocklebank sits and they help themselves to drinks from a bottle of whisky from the bottom of the filing cabinet

Brocklebank I do hope she's all right, the little minx.
Bernard So Operation Tyger Tyger draws to its conclusion.
Brocklebank Yup. What are you doing next?
Bernard A spot of money-laundering by the sound of things — some naughty little pixies in Buenos Aires. And you?
Brocklebank God knows.
Bernard Who's a gloomy bunny? Mission accomplished: the Surgeon is dead.
Brocklebank Yes, his time is up.
Bernard I owe you an apology, George. I never really thought it was Collingwood. I trusted him — we used to play squash together in Haywards Heath.
Brocklebank Perhaps you thought it was me — that I was the Surgeon?

Bernard shrugs

It could only have been one of us in the final analysis.

Bernard Hence the trap. The trap to trap the trapper.

Brocklebank So she had no choice in the end, little Zoë — she had to shoot him.

Bernard Thank God we didn't give her the blanks after all.

Brocklebank Yes, indeed, thank God. I did want to see the bastard in the dock though. I've been denied that.

Bernard "O judgement! thou art fled to brutish beasts
And men have lost their reason."

Brocklebank (*dismissing Bernard*) I'll see you tomorrow.

Bernard *Julius Caesar.* Good-night.

Bernard exits

Left alone, Brocklebank reflects on his position. He is a troubled man. He takes a long swig of booze

Brocklebank's mobile rings

Brocklebank (*into the mobile*) Hallo. ... Zoë? Where the hell are you? We've been looking for you. ... Because we're concerned about you, my dear. ... Me especially. ... (*He paces about*) What sort of a remark is that? Are you trying to tell me something, because if so we must arrange to meet. ... What do you mean "No sooner said than done" — where are you?

Zoë enters at the back of the auditorium. She is speaking into her mobile and carries a remote control. She and Brocklebank continue to speak to each other on their mobiles during the following

Zoë (*on her mobile*) Haven't you realized yet that it's a trait of mine, to take the battle to the enemy? To beard the lion in his den. It usually pays off.

Brocklebank (*on his mobile*) Not the enemy, surely? If you want to talk things over, that's fine by me.

Zoë (*on her mobile*) I'm so glad, George.

Brocklebank (*on his mobile*) After all, you must be feeling somewhat debilitated.

Zoë (*on her mobile*) Not so much debilitated as curious. You can hang up now — those things aren't good for you.

Brocklebank wheels round and sees Zoë in the auditorium. He is surprised to see her

Brocklebank (*recovering his cool*) How the hell did you get in here?

Zoë disconnects her mobile. Brocklebank does too

Zoë The daily security codes follow a predictable sequence. You said yourself that I wasn't stupid.

From her position in the auditorium, Zoë switches a spotlight on Brocklebank with the remote, as he did to her at the beginning

Brocklebank What are you doing?
Zoë It's not an audition this time. I want to talk to you, George, privately.
Brocklebank What about?
Zoë The Surgeon.
Brocklebank Yes, well, we may not have got the result we wanted but at least you're safe.
Zoë What was the result we wanted?
Brocklebank Our objective was to arrest him and prosecute him in a court of law.
Zoë So it was. The press have dubbed you a hero. How do you like that?
Brocklebank (*about the light*) Why don't you turn that thing off and come down and talk to me.

The Light remains trained on him at the table. Zoë comes forward on to the stage

Zoë I want to get things straight in my mind before I give my formal statement. Let's just scroll back a bit and see if I've got things right.
Brocklebank Are you sure that's a good idea? Isn't it getting rather late?
Zoë We're perfectly alone and I have no pressing engagements — do you?
Brocklebank No. Shall we sit down? (*He sits*)

Zoë switches off the spotlight and paces around during the following

Zoë So there you are, George, in the eyes of the world, the heroic if maverick cop who oh-so-nearly got his man — but alas, the young bimbo screwed up and shot the suspect.
Brocklebank I'm trying to see where you're going with this. Are you all right?
Zoë I'm fine, thanks. (*Pause*) But there's another, quite different, scenario trundling round inside my head ... May I?
Brocklebank Please. All this melodrama ... I think what you need is a holiday.

Zoë Good idea. Now let's go back to the point where the investigation began to focus on the possibility that, horror of horrors, the Surgeon was actually a policeman himself. A solitary psychotic buried somewhere deep in the heart of the police force.

Brocklebank Florid prose indeed.

Zoë Bear with me.

Brocklebank (*nodding*) This is your party.

Zoë Picture, if you will, the Surgeon as a highly-respected police officer, who suspects that the net is closing in on him.

Brocklebank I'm all ears.

Zoë Somehow he manoeuvres himself into the key position of investigating *his own crimes*.

Brocklebank Oh, Zoë …

Zoë He is perfectly placed to divert attention from himself. He even goes one step further and decides to actually deliver "the culprit".

Brocklebank And how does he pull that off?

Zoë In the best tradition of double play — he pits two sides against the middle. He takes on the role of impresario.

Brocklebank (*laughing*) What are you on, young lady?

Zoë He sets up poor Collingwood in the role of the prime suspect and then hires a young girl to play the part of a decoy.

Brocklebank How on earth did he pull that one off?

Zoë He tells Collingwood it's a a very detailed training exercise. It's the kind of thing Jerry is good at. The girl is there because she needs the dosh.

Brocklebank Very convenient. So then what happens?

Zoë Obviously you didn't want Collingwood taken alive, so the girl is primed, or allowed, rather, to shoot Collingwood. The recordings will show that it was a clear case of self-defence.

Brocklebank Wow. It's so obvious I can't think how we missed it.

Zoë The evidence is all neatly stacked up and the inquiry is closed. The Surgeon is dead. Bravo for George.

Brocklebank Zoë, look enough is enough. This is a lot of half-baked nonsense. You haven't got one shred of evidence for any of this. If I wasn't so fond of you I'd be quite hurt.

Zoë I haven't finished.

Brocklebank What now? An invasion of aliens?

Zoë It was all faked. The shot that I fired at Collingwood was a blank.

Brocklebank Well, stap mi vitals! How come he's in the morgue then?

Zoë That's where you were so clever. On the one hand you got me to shoot him and on the other you persuaded Collingwood to play dead. With hindsight in fact he was a bit too willing.

Brocklebank To what purpose, though?

Zoë So that once I've gone, he gets off the floor having completed his part in what he thinks is a successful training mission. But what does he get?
Brocklebank You tell me, clever clogs.
Zoë Another bullet. A real one. You shoot him. As per your plan.
Brocklebank It's a cumbersome theory. (*He circles round Zoë*) But surely as the Surgeon I am too cunning to have left any clues?
Zoë Yes, the girl is the problem — she's bright, remember? At her original assessment for the job she scored forty-two out of a possible fifty. She did particularly well in improvisation, remember?
Brocklebank We estimated she was volatile due to the damage she suffered ... (*he taunts her*) as a child at the hands of her Uncle Gareth.
Zoë Shut up. That's something else I'll never forgive you for.
Brocklebank So what is the magical piece of evidence she thinks she's got?
Zoë She's not going to tell him, is she, alone late at night in an empty lecture hall ...
Brocklebank Then he has to decide if she's bluffing or not.
Zoë As always, the sporting metaphor.
Brocklebank Either way he has got to kill her, hasn't he?
Zoë You don't imagine she has covered her arse, then?
Brocklebank Knowing her I'd say she arrived unprepared.
Zoë Perhaps that's his biggest mistake: underestimating the people in his command.
Brocklebank Zoë, Zoë, Zoë ...
Zoë So he thinks he's quite safe?
Brocklebank (*squatting at Zoë's side*) I don't think he wants to kill her. Not if he has a choice ... So tell me, sweetheart, what evidence do you think you've got?
Zoë OK ... Let's go back to the moment Collingwood realizes you've doubled crossed him — with your gun in his face all he can do is pick up his mobile and hit the last recall button.
Brocklebank The last recall button?
Zoë Which puts him through to my message service. (*Pause*) Which records in very good quality (*pause*) a very damning conversation (*pause*) between Detective Inspector Jerry Collingwood and yourself. (*Pause*) Every last word recorded. Including the shot that killed him. Horribly loud.
Brocklebank Oh, dear. That does rather alter things.

Brocklebank moves behind Zoë with electric speed, produces a silk tie and slips it round her neck. She is transfixed

Zoë I always knew it was you.
Brocklebank Oh, yes? Don't tell me it was feminine intuition?

Zoë Something like that. There's a lot to be learnt about a man from a kiss.
Brocklebank I wondered about that. What did you learn about me, Miss
Lang with no "I"?
Zoë Your breath smells. It stinks. It was a kiss of death …

*They have a brief struggle. Brocklebank remains in control, trapping her
with his tie, either pinioning her on to the desk or holding her from behind,
sitting in the chair*

Brocklebank Shut up, shut up, Zoë. What the hell am I going to do with you?
Zoë We've ruled out pleading for mercy or bribery then?
Brocklebank Don't be stupid, we're well beyond that. It's all got to stop
now, I suppose. What a shame.

*Zoë reaches for the camera and manages to activate it so that we see
Brocklebank's face on the screen — the Surgeon in hideous close-up*

Zoë Traditionally this is where you tell me what it was all about?
Brocklebank Who knows where these things start? I could tell you I've been
corrupted by the things I've seen in my work. (*He reflects*) But the truth is,
it has always been there inside me, the excitement of it … All that frenzied
struggling for breath, the veins standing out and the eyes — the spasms and
then the lovely calm as they yield — and afterwards the stainless steel
going through the flesh — like a knife through butter … (*After a reverie*)
It's a question of taking out the poisonous core, you see. They always said
there's no passion in the way I treated my victims … What do they know?
What do they know of that moment as the life force ebbs from those silly
girls. And the poem made it all so beautiful … (*He whispers*) Do it with me
Zoë … For one last time … "Tyger, Tyger." Please …
Zoë
Brocklebank } (*roughly in unison*) "When the stars threw down their spears
And watered Heaven with their tears:
Did he smile his work to see?
Did he who made the Lamb make thee?"

Bernard enters at the back of the auditorium with a pistol

Bernard (*shouting*) Stop. Don't move. *Stop.* Right there.

Bernard moves to the stage

Let her go. Zoë, are you all right?
Zoë (*moving to Bernard*) I never thought I'd be so glad to see you, Bernard.
Brocklebank The Surgeon has to be stopped, doesn't he, Bernard?

Bernard (*shielding Zoë*) Yes, he does.
Brocklebank I've rather let the side down, haven't I?
Bernard The case is closed. You've nowhere left to go.

Bernard puts the pistol on the desk in front of Brocklebank and pushes it towards him

Brocklebank (*understanding his duty*) Oh I see … Thank you.
Bernard Come on, Zoë …

Bernard and Zoë exit through the automatic door

As the door closes, Brocklebank picks up the pistol. As he speaks he turns the pistol towards his mouth

The Lights begin to fade

Brocklebank "Did he smile his work to see?
        Did he who made the Lamb make thee?"

Black-out. There is a loud gunshot

FURNITURE AND PROPERTY LIST

ACT I

SCENE 1

On stage: Desks
Chairs
Filing cabinets
Telephones
Fridge. *In it:* bottle of water
Recording console
Large practical television monitor (or two smaller ones) linked to practical video camera (and with video playback facility)
Practical speakers
Other technical devices and remote controls
Files, including: documentation with photograph of **Brocklebank**; **Bernard**'s paperwork; **Zoë**'s papers; other files of photographs and news cuttings including highlighted advertisement from a contact magazine; very distinctive file; fat folder containing Natasha Campion's details
Clipboard and pen for **Bernard**
Pad of Post-It notes

Personal: **Bernard**: mobile phone

SCENE 2

On stage: As ACT I Scene1

Personal: **Zoë**: bag containing Natasha's mobile phone
Brocklebank: small box containing tiny radio microphone in the shape of a brooch

SCENE 3

On stage: Cupboards
Chairs
Table. *On it*: folder containing script. *In drawer*: cassette
Sound system (practical)
Note
Gladstone bag. *In it:* white cloth, sealed transparent plastic bag full of offal

Off stage: Wet umbrella (**Zoë**)
                Second copy of script (**John Smith**)
                Ready-poured drink (**John Smith**)

Personal: **John Smith**: knife

ACT II

Scene 1

On stage: As ACT I Scene 2 (perhaps tidied slightly)

Set: Brooch microphone
          In desk drawer: container holding small revolver
          Mobile phone for **Bernard**

Off stage: **Bernard**: cup of herb tea

Personal: **Zoë**: bag containing teabag and Natasha's mobile phone
          Brocklebank: bottle of pills

Scene 2

On stage: Cupboards
          Chairs
          Table. *On it*: glass of water, **John Smith**'s mobile phone
          Sound system (practical)
          Key in door

Personal: **John Smith**: silk tie, blood capsule
          Brocklebank: silencer, communication device

Scene 3

On stage: As ACT II Scene 1

Set: Drinks
          Glasses

Off stage: Mobile phone, remote control (**Zoë**)

Personal: **Brocklebank**: silk tie
          Bernard: pistol

LIGHTING PLOT

Practical fittings required: nil
Two interiors

ACT I, SCENE 1

To open: Darkness

Cue 1   Single set of footsteps approaches   (Page 1)
             Bring up general interior lighting

Cue 2   **Brocklebank** touches a switch   (Page 4)
             Bring up spotlight on **Zoë**

Cue 3   Buzzer goes off   (Page 6)
             Cut spotlight

Cue 4   **Brocklebank** laughs and disconnects the phone   (Page 14)
             Fade lights to black-out

ACT I, SCENE 2

To open: Darkness

Cue 5   As video proceeds   (Page 14)
             Bring up general interior lighting

Cue 6   **Brocklebank**: "… made the Lamb make thee?"   (Page 23)
             Black-out

ACT I, SCENE 3

To open: Darkness

Cue 7   **John Smith** (voice-over): " … and then the Yale." (Page 23)
             *Bring up dim general interior lighting with rain effect
             and flashes of lightning outside; continue throughout scene*

Cue 8   **Zoë** turns the lights on   (Page 23)
             Bring up feeble overhead lights

Lighting Plot

Cue 9   **Zoë** closes the curtains and goes to the door   (Page 24)
          Bring up dim torchlight through the curtains

ACT II, SCENE 1

To open: General interior lighting

Cue 11   **Bernard**: *"Que sera sera ..."*   (Page 44)
          Black-out

ACT II, SCENE 2

To open: General interior lighting

Cue 12   **John Smith**: "What the hammer ... ?"   (Page 45)
          Fade lights to black-out during following speech

Cue 13   **John Smith**: " ... deadly terrors grasp?"   (Page 45)
          Pause. Bring up general interior lighting

Cue 14   Sounds of police activity outside   (Page 49)
          Blue flashing light

Cue 15   **Zoë** unlocks and opens the door   (Page 49)
          Blue flashing light

Cue 16   **Brocklebank**: " ... and ambulance here immediately ..."   (Page 52)
          Black-out

ACT II, SCENE 3

To open: Darkness

Cue 17   Telephone rings   (Page 53)
          Bring up general interior lighting

Cue 18   **Zoë** presses a button on the remote   (Page 55)
          Bring up spotlight on **Brocklebank**

Cue 19   **Zoë** switches off the spotlight   (Page 55)
          Cut spotlight

Cue 20   **Brocklebank** picks up the pistol   (Page 59)
          Fade to black-out during the following

EFFECTS PLOT

ACT I

Cue 1 When ready   (Page 1)
Two sets of footsteps with echo; door clangs; single set of footsteps

Cue 2 **Zoë**: 'The Seventies rock group ..."   (Page 6)
Buzzer

Cue 3 **Brocklebank**: "She must be ready."   (Page 17)
Buzzer

Cue 4 **Zoë**: "Bog off."   (Page 19)
Mobile rings. Activate microphone offstage
   so following dialogue comes from onstage speakers

Cue 5 **John Smith**: "Bye-bye."   (Page 20)
Sound of phone being hung up. De-activate offstage microphone

Cue 6 **Brocklebank**: "... the Lamb make thee?" (Page 23)
Sound of heavy rain and distant thunder;
   continue throughout scene

Cue 7 **John Smith** presses a button on the sound system (Page 28)
   "Volare, Nel Blu di Punto di Blu" by Dean Martin plays

Cue 8 **John Smith** turns the music off   (Page 29)
Cut music

Cue 9 **Zoë**: "Yes indeed."   (Page 29)
Increase volume of thunder noises to end of scene

Cue 10 **John Smith**: " ... over your grave ...?" *(Page 30)*
Zoë'*s mobile phone rings*

Cue 11 **John Smith** tears up **Zoë**'s script   (Page 31)
Loud rumble of thunder

Cue 12 The contents of the bag spill out   (Page 32)
Clap of thunder

ACT II

Cue 13 When ready   (Page 33)
Zoë'*s scream from end of ACT 1 Scene 3*

Effects Plot

Cue 14	**Bernard** rewinds the tape and presses "Play" *Taped dialogue as pp.33-34*	(Page 33)
Cue 15	**Brocklebank**: " … poke my Biro up your nose." *Telephone rings*	(Page 34)
Cue 16	**Brocklebank**: "… your quota for today." *Entryphone buzzes. Activate offstage microphone*	(Page 35)
Cue 17	**Zoë**: "Open the door." *De-activate offstage microphone*	(Page 36)
Cue 18	**Bernard** presses a button *Taped dialogue as p. 37*	(Page 37)
Cue 19	**Brocklebank** activates the tape machine *Taped dialogue as pp. 38-39*	(Page 38)
Cue 20	**Brocklebank** switches off the tape *Cut taped dialogue*	(Page 39)
Cue 21	**Brocklebank**: "Maybe it has." *Mobile rings*	(Page 39)
Cue 22	**Zoë** answers the mobile *Activate microphone off stage so following dialogue comes from onstage speakers*	(Page 40)
Cue 23	**Brocklebank** terminates the call *De-activate offstage microphone*	(Page 41)
Cue 24	Loud knocking on the door *Police sirens in distance*	(Page 48)
Cue 25	**Zoë**: "This isn't an acting exercise … ?" *Police activity outside*	(Page 49)
Cue 26	Black-out *Taped **Newsreader**'s speech as p.52*	(Page 52)
Cue 27	During **Newsreader**'s speech *Phone rings*	(Page 52)
Cue 28	**Bernard** turns off the radio news *Cut **Newsreader**'s speech*	(Page 53)
Cue 29	**Brocklebank** takes a long swig of booze **Brocklebank**'s *mobile phone rings*	(Page 54)
Cue 30	Black-out *Gunshot*	(Page 59)

VIDEO PLOT

Cue 1   As ACT 1 Scene 2 begins   (Page 14)
             Video of **Zoë** *on screen(s) — script as p.14*

THE FIREARMS (AMENDMENT) BILL

Samuel French is grateful to Charles Vance, Vice-Chairman of the Theatres Advisory Council, for the following information regarding the Firearms (Amendment) Bill:

"The Firearms (Amendment) Bill does not affect blank-firing pistols which are not readily convertible (i.e. those which do not require a Firearms Certificate). Among the reasons against imposing restrictions on such items is their use in theatre, cinema and television as a "safe" alternative to real guns.

The general prohibition on the possession of real handguns will apply to those used for theatrical purposes. It would clearly be anomalous to prohibit the use of those items for target shooting, but permit their use for purposes where a fully-working gun is not needed. As handguns will become "Section 5" prohibited weapons, they would fall under the same arrangements as at present apply to real machine guns. As you will know, there are companies which are authorized by the Secretary of State to supply such weapons for theatrical purposes.

The exemption under Section 12 of the Firearms Act 1968, whereby actors can use firearms without themselves having a Firearms Certificate, will remain in force".

Regulations apply to the United Kingdom only. Producers in other countries should refer to appropriate legislation.